CHINA IN THE 21ST CENTURY

CHINA

ECONOMIC CONDITIONS AND RELIABILITY OF ECONOMIC DATA

China in the 21st Century

Additional books in this series can be found on Nova's website under the Series tab.

Additional E-books in this series can be found on Nova's website under the E-book tab.

CHINA IN THE 21ST CENTURY

CHINA

ECONOMIC CONDITIONS AND RELIABILITY OF ECONOMIC DATA

HEATHER A. COLLINS
EDITOR

New York

For permission to use material from this book please contact us:
Telephone 631-231-7269; Fax 631-231-8175
Web Site: http://www.novapublishers.com

Additional color graphics may be available in the e-book version of this book.

Library of Congress Cataloging-in-Publication Data

ISBN: 978-1-62618-536-4

Published by Nova Science Publishers, Inc. † New York

CONTENTS

PREFACE

Prior to the initiation of economic reforms and trade liberalization 33 years ago, China maintained policies that kept the economy very poor, stagnant, centrally controlled, vastly inefficient, and relatively isolated from the global economy. Since opening up to foreign trade and investment and implementing free market reforms in 1979, China has been among the world's fastest-growing economies, with real annual gross domestic product (GDP) averaging nearly 10% through 2011. In recent years, China has emerged as a major global economic and trade power. It is currently the world's second-largest economy, largest merchandise exporter, second-largest merchandise importer, second-largest destination of foreign-direct investment (FDI), largest manufacturer, largest holder of foreign exchange reserves, and largest creditor nation. This book provides background on China's economic rise; describes its current economic structure; identifies the challenges China faces to keep its economy growing strong; and discusses the challenges, opportunities, and implications of China's economic rise for the United States.

Chapter 1 - This chapter provides background on China's economic rise; describes its current economic structure; identifies the challenges China faces to keep its economy growing strong; and discusses the challenges, opportunities, and implications of China's economic rise for the United States.

Chapter 2 - This chapter focuses on China's national output statistics, or gross domestic product (GDP). It concludes that China's official statistics are not as reliable as those produced in the United States and Europe. Several findings support this conclusion. The first is that there are serious deficiencies in the way the Chinese government gathers, measures, and presents its data. Although China's National Bureau of Statistics (NBS) now uses sample surveys to measure the economy, survey coverage remains incomplete, particularly in services and the private sector. Economic censuses, in turn, prompt inordinately large revisions of statistical data, and are themselves not on par with international standards. At the same time, many industrial enterprises still report their output directly to the government, keeping in place a Soviet-style reporting system based on state-owned enterprises.

In: China
Editor: Heather A. Collins
ISBN: 978-1-62618-536-4

Chapter 1

CHINA'S ECONOMIC CONDITIONS*

Wayne M. Morrison

SUMMARY

Prior to the initiation of economic reforms and trade liberalization 33 years ago, China maintained policies that kept the economy very poor, stagnant, centrally controlled, vastly inefficient, and relatively isolated from the global economy. Since opening up to foreign trade and investment and implementing free market reforms in 1979, China has been among the world's fastest-growing economies, with real annual gross domestic product (GDP) averaging nearly 10% through 2011. In recent years, China has emerged as a major global economic and trade power. It is currently the world's second-largest economy, largest merchandise exporter, second-largest merchandise importer, second-largest destination of foreign direct investment (FDI), largest manufacturer, largest holder of foreign exchange reserves, and largest creditor nation.

The global economic crisis that began in 2008 greatly affected China's economy. China's exports, imports, and FDI inflows declined, GDP growth slowed, and millions of Chinese workers reportedly lost their jobs. The Chinese government responded by implementing a $586 billion economic stimulus package, loosening monetary policies to increase bank lending, and providing various incentives to boost domestic

* This is an edited, reformatted and augmented version of Congressional Research Service, Publication No. RL33534, dated December 4, 2012.

consumption. Such policies enabled China to effectively weather the effects of the sharp global fall in demand for Chinese products, while several of the world's leading economies experienced negative or stagnant economic growth. From 2008 to 2011, China's real GDP growth averaged 9.6%, although it has slowed somewhat in 2012.

Some economic forecasters project that China will overtake the United States as the world's largest economy within a few years, although U.S. per capita GDP levels are expected to remain much larger than those of China for many years to come. However, the ability of China to maintain a rapidly growing economy in the long run will depend largely on the ability of the Chinese government to implement comprehensive economic reforms that more quickly hasten China's transition to a free market economy; rebalance the Chinese economy by making consumer demand, rather than exporting and fixed investment, the main engine of economic growth; and boosting productivity and innovation. China faces numerous other challenges as well that could affect its future economic growth, such as widespread pollution, growing income disparities, an undeveloped social safety net, and extensive involvement of the state in the economy. The Chinese government has acknowledged that its current economic growth model needs to be altered. In October 2006, the Chinese government formally outlined a goal of building a "harmonious socialist society" by taking steps (by 2020) to lessen income inequality, improve the rule of law, enhance environmental protection, reduce corruption, and improve the country's social safety net (such as expanding health care and pension coverage to rural areas). In addition, the government announced plans to rebalance the economy and boost innovation.

China's economic rise has significant implications for the United States and hence is of major interest to Congress. On the one hand, China is a large (and potentially huge) export market for the United States. Many U.S. firms use China as the final point of assembly in their global supply chain networks. China's large holdings of U.S. Treasury securities help the federal government finance its budget deficits and keep U.S. interest rates low. However, some analysts contend that China maintains a number of distortive economic policies (such as an undervalued currency and protectionist industrial policies) that undermine U.S. economic interests. They warn that efforts by the Chinese government to promote innovation could mean that Chinese firms will increasingly pose a "competitive challenge" to many leading U.S. industries. This report surveys the rise of China's economy, describes major economic challenges facing China, and discusses the challenges, opportunities, and implications of China's economic rise for the United States.

The rapid rise of China as a major economic power within a time span of about three decades is often described by analysts as one of the greatest economic success stories in modern times. From 1979 (when economic reforms began) to 2011, China's real gross domestic product (GDP) grew at an average annual rate of nearly 10%.[1] From 1980 to 2011, real GDP grew 19-fold in real terms, real per capita GDP increased 14-fold, and an estimated 500 million people were raised out of extreme poverty. China is now the world's second-largest economy and some analysts predict it could become the largest within a few years. Yet, on a per capita basis, China remains a relatively poor country.

China's economic rise has led to a substantial increase in U.S.-China economic ties. According to U.S. trade data, total trade between the two countries surged from $5 billion in 1980 to $503 billion in 2011. China is currently the United States' second-largest trading partner, its third-largest export market, and its largest source of imports. Many U.S. companies have extensive operations in China in order to sell their products in the booming Chinese market and to take advantage of lower-cost labor for export-oriented manufacturing.[2] These operations have helped some U.S. firms to remain internationally competitive and have supplied U.S. consumers with a variety of low-cost goods. China's large-scale purchases of U.S. Treasury securities (which totaled nearly $1.2 trillion at the end of 2011) have enabled the federal government to fund its budget deficits, which help keep U.S. interest rates relatively low.

However, the emergence of China as a major economic superpower has raised concern among many U.S. policymakers. Some claim that China uses unfair trade practices (such as an undervalued currency and subsidies given to domestic producers) to flood U.S. markets with low-cost goods, and that such practices threaten American jobs, wages, and living standards. Others contend that China's growing use of industrial policies to promote and protect certain domestic Chinese industries firms favored by the government, and its failure to take effective action against widespread infringement of U.S. intellectual property rights (IPR) in China, threaten to undermine the competitiveness of U.S. IP-intensive industries. In addition, while China has become a large and growing market for U.S. exports, critics contend that numerous trade and investment barriers limit opportunities for U.S. firms to sell in China, or force them to set up production facilities in China as the price of doing business there. Other concerns relating to China's economic growth include its growing demand for energy and raw materials and its emergence as the world's largest emitter of greenhouse gasses.

The Chinese government views a growing economy as vital to maintaining social stability. However, China faces a number of major economic challenges which could undermine future growth, including distortive economic policies that have resulted in over-reliance on fixed investment and exports for economic growth (rather than on consumer demand), government support for state-owned firms, a weak banking system, widening income gaps, growing pollution, and the relative lack of the rule of law in China. Many economists warn that such problems could undermine China's future economic growth. The Chinese government has acknowledged these problems and has pledged to address them by implementing policies to boost consumer spending, expand social safety net coverage, and encourage the development of less-polluting industries.

This report provides background on China's economic rise; describes its current economic structure; identifies the challenges China faces to keep its economy growing strong; and discusses the challenges, opportunities, and implications of China's economic rise for the United States.

THE HISTORY OF CHINA'S ECONOMIC DEVELOPMENT

China's Economy Prior to Reforms

Prior to 1979, China, under the leadership of Chairman Mao Zedong, maintained a centrally planned, or command, economy. A large share of the country's economic output was directed and controlled by the state, which set production goals, controlled prices, and allocated resources throughout most of the economy. During the 1950s, all of China's individual household farms were collectivized into large communes. To support rapid industrialization, the central government undertook large-scale investments in physical and human capital during the 1960s and 1970s. As a result, by 1978 nearly three-fourths of industrial production was produced by centrally controlled, state-owned enterprises (SOEs), according to centrally planned output targets. Private enterprises and foreign-invested firms were generally barred. A central goal of the Chinese government was to make China's economy relatively self-sufficient. Foreign trade was generally limited to obtaining only those goods that could not be made or obtained in China.

Government policies kept the Chinese economy relatively stagnant and inefficient, mainly because most aspects of the economy were managed and run by the central government (and thus there were few profit incentives for firms, workers, and farmers), competition was virtually nonexistent, foreign trade and investment flows were mainly limited to Soviet bloc countries, and price and production controls caused widespread distortions in the economy. Chinese living standards were substantially lower than those of many other developing countries. The Chinese government in 1978 (shortly after the death of Chairman Mao in 1976) decided to break with its Soviet-style economic policies by gradually reforming the economy according to free market principles and opening up trade and investment with the West, in the hope that this would significantly increase economic growth and raise living standards. As Chinese leader Deng Xiaoping, the architect of China's economic reforms, put it: "Black cat, white cat, what does it matter what color the cat is as long as it catches mice?"[3]

The Introduction of Economic Reforms

Beginning in 1979, China launched several economic reforms. The central government initiated price and ownership incentives for farmers, which enabled them to sell a portion of their crops on the free market. In addition, the government established four special economic zones along the coast for the purpose of attracting foreign investment, boosting exports, and importing high technology products into China. Additional reforms, which followed in stages, sought to decentralize economic policymaking in several sectors, especially trade. Economic control of various enterprises was given to provincial and local governments, which were generally allowed to operate and compete on free market principles, rather than under the direction and guidance of state planning. In addition, citizens were encouraged to start their own businesses. Additional coastal regions and cities were designated as open cities and development zones, which allowed them to experiment with free market reforms and to offer tax and trade incentives to attract foreign investment. In addition, state price controls on a wide range of products were gradually eliminated. Trade liberalization was also a major key to China's economic success. Removing trade barriers encouraged greater competition and attracted foreign direct investment (FDI) inflows.[4] China's gradual implementation of economic reforms sought to identify which policies produced favorable economic outcomes (and which did not) so that they could be implemented in other parts of the country, a process Deng Xiaoping reportedly referred to as "crossing the river by touching the stones."[5]

China's Economic Growth Since Reforms: 1979-2012

Since the introduction of economic reforms, China's economy has grown substantially faster than during the pre-reform period (see **Table 1**). According to the Chinese government, from 1953 to 1978, real annual GDP growth was estimated at 6.7%,[6] although many analysts claim that Chinese economic data during this period are highly questionable because government officials often exaggerated production levels for a variety of political reasons.[7] Agnus Maddison estimates China's average annual real GDP during this period at 4.4%.[8]

China's economy suffered economic downturns during the leadership of Chairman Mao Zedong, including during the Great Leap Forward from 1958 to 1960 (which led to a massive famine and reportedly the deaths of tens of millions of people) and the Cultural Revolution from 1966 to 1976 (which caused political chaos and greatly disrupted the economy). During the reform period (1979-2011), China's average annual real GDP grew by 9.9%. This essentially has meant that, on average China has been able to double the size of its economy in real terms every eight years.

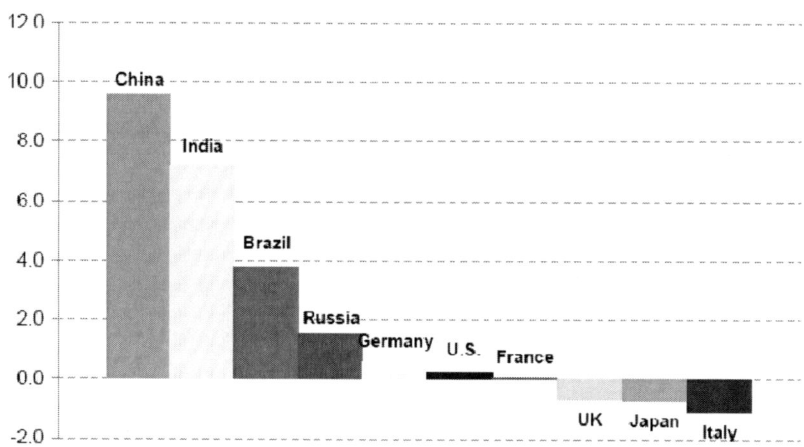

Source: EIU database.

Figure 1. Average Real GDP Growth Among Major Global Economies: 2008-2011; (percent).

The global economic slowdown, which began in 2008, impacted the Chinese economy (especially the export sector). China's real GDP growth fell from 14.2% in 2007 to 9.6% in 2008 to 9.2% in 2009. In response, the Chinese government implemented a large economic stimulus package and an expansive monetary policy. These measures boosted domestic investment and consumption and helped prevent a sharp economic slowdown in China. In 2010, China's real GDP grew by 10.4%, and in 2011 it rose by 9.2%. The International Monetary Fund (IMF) projects that China's real GDP will grow by 7.8% in 2012. From 2013 to 2017, the IMP projects that China's real GDP growth will average 8.5%.

Table 1. China's Average Annual Real GDP Growth: 1979-2012

Year	Real Growth Rate (%)
1979	7.6
1980	7.9
1981	5.3
1982	9.0
1983	10.9
1984	15.2
1985	13.5
1986	8.9
1987	11.6
1988	11.3
1989	4.1
1990	3.8
1991	9.2
1992	14.2
1993	13.9
1994	13.1
1995	10.9
1996	10.0
1997	9.3
1998	7.8
1999	7.6
2000	8.4
2001	8.3
2002	9.1
2003	10.0
2004	10.1
2005	11.3
2006	12.7
2007	14.2
2008	9.6
2009	9.2
2010	10.4
2011	9.2
2012 IMF projection	7.8

Source: Economist Intelligence Unit and IMF.

Causes of China's Economic Growth

Economists generally attribute much of China's rapid economic growth to two main factors: large-scale capital investment (financed by large domestic savings and foreign investment) and rapid productivity growth. These two factors appear to have gone together hand in hand. Economic reforms led to higher efficiency in the economy, which boosted output and increased resources for additional investment in the economy.

China has historically maintained a high rate of savings. When reforms were initiated in 1979, domestic savings as a percentage of GDP stood at 32%. However, most Chinese savings during this period were generated by the profits of SOEs, which were used by the central government for domestic investment. Economic reforms, which included the decentralization of economic production, led to substantial growth in Chinese household savings as well as corporate savings. As a result, China's gross savings as a percentage of GDP has steadily risen, reaching 53.9% in 2010 (compared to a U.S. rate of 9.3%), and is among the highest savings rates in the world.[9] The large level of savings has enabled China to boost domestic investment. In fact, its gross domestic savings levels far exceed its domestic investment levels, meaning that China is a large net global lender. Several economists have concluded that productivity gains (i.e., increases in efficiency) have been another major factor in China's rapid economic growth. The improvements to productivity were caused largely by a reallocation of resources to more productive uses, especially in sectors that were formerly heavily controlled by the central government, such as agriculture, trade, and services. For example, agricultural reforms boosted production, freeing workers to pursue employment in the more productive manufacturing sector. China's decentralization of the economy led to the rise of non-state enterprises (such as private firms), which tended to pursue more productive activities than the centrally controlled SOEs and were more market-oriented, and hence, more efficient. Additionally, a greater share of the economy (mainly the export sector) was exposed to competitive forces. Local and provincial governments were allowed to establish and operate various enterprises on market principles, without interference from the central government. In addition, FDI in China brought with it new technology and processes that boosted efficiency. As indicated in **Figure 2**, China has achieved high rates of total factor productivity (TFP) growth relative to the United States. TFP represents an estimate of the part of economic output growth not accounted for by the growth in inputs (such as labor and capital), and is often attributed to the effects of technological change and efficiency gains. China experiences faster TFP growth than most developed countries such as the United States because of its ability to access and utilize existing foreign technology and know-how. High TFP growth rates have been a major factor behind China's rapid economic growth rate. However, as China's technological development begins to approach that of major developed countries, its level of productivity gains, and thus, real GDP growth, could slow significantly from its historic 10% average, unless China becomes a major center for new technology and innovation and/or implements new comprehensive economic reforms.[10] As indicated in **Figure 3**, the EIU currently projects that China's real GDP growth will slow considerably in the years ahead, averaging 7.0% from 2012 to 2020, and falling to 3.7% from 2021 to 2030.[11] The Chinese government has indicated its desire to move away from its current economic model of fast growth at any cost to more "smart" economic growth, which seeks to reduce reliance on energy-intensive and high-polluting industries and rely more on high technology, green energy, and services. China also has indicated it wants to obtain more balanced economic growth. (These issues are discussedin more detail later in the report.)

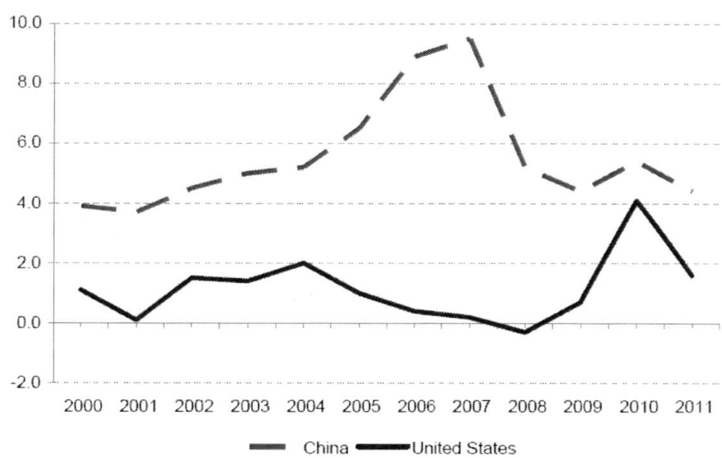

Source: Estimated by the Economist Intelligence Unit.

Note: Total factor productivity represents the part of economic output growth not accounted for by the growth in inputs, such as labor and capital, and is often used to estimate the effects of technological change.

Figure 2. Comparison of Annual Changes in Total Factor Productivity in China and the United States: 2000-2011; (percent).

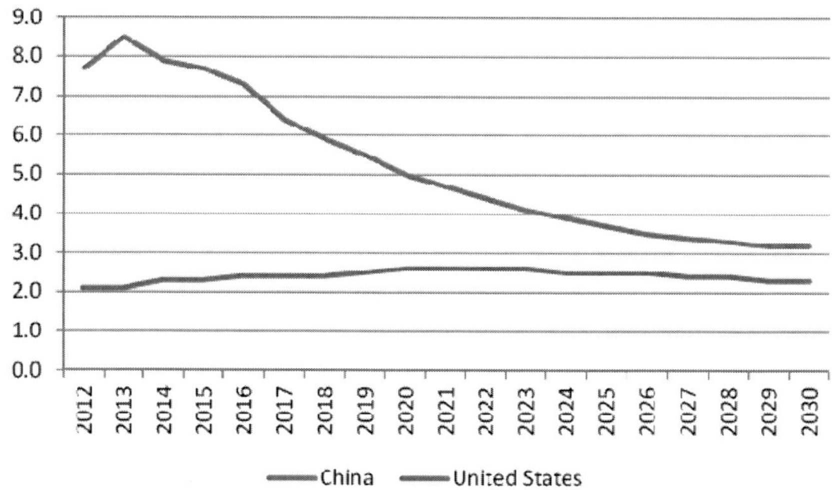

Source: Economist Intelligence Unit.
Note: Long-range economic projections should be viewed with caution.

Figure 3. Projections of U.S. and Chinese Real GDP Growth Rates: 2012-2030; (percent).

MEASURING THE SIZE OF CHINA'S ECONOMY

The rapid growth of the Chinese economy has led many analysts to speculate if and when China will overtake the United States as the "world's largest economic power." The "actual" size of China's economy has been a subject of extensive debate among economists. Measured in U.S. dollars using nominal exchange rates, China's GDP in 2011 was $7.2 trillion, less than half the size of the U.S. economy.[12] The per capita GDP (a common measurement of a country's living standards) of China was $5,460, which was 12% the size of Japan's level and 11% that of the United States (see Table 2).

Many economists contend that using nominal exchange rates to convert Chinese data (or that of other countries) into U.S. dollars fails to reflect the true size of China's economy and living standards relative to the United States. Nominal exchange rates simply reflect the prices of foreign currencies vis-à-vis the U.S. dollar and such measurements exclude differences in the prices for goods and services across countries. To illustrate, one U.S. dollar exchanged for local currency in China would buy more goods and services there than it would in the United States. This is because prices for goods and services in

China are generally lower than they are in the United States. Conversely, prices for goods and services in Japan are generally higher than they are in the United States (and China). Thus, one dollar exchanged for local Japanese currency would buy fewer goods and services there than it would in the United States. Economists attempt to develop estimates of exchange rates based on their actual purchasing power relative to the dollar in order to make more accurate comparisons of economic data across countries, usually referred to as a purchasing power parity (PPP) basis. The PPP exchange rate increases the (estimated) measurement of China's economy and its per capita GDP. According to the Economist Intelligence Unit, (EIU), which utilizes World Bank data, prices for goods and services in China are 41.5% the level they are in the United States. Adjusting for this price differential raises the value of China's 2011 GDP from $7.2 trillion (nominal dollars) to $11.4 trillion (on a PPP basis).[13] This would indicate that China's economy is 76.0% the size of the U.S. economy. China's share of global GDP on a PPP basis rose from 3.7% in 1990 to 14.3% in 2011 (the U.S. share of global GDP peaked at 24.3% in 1999 and declined to 18.9% in 2011); see Figure 4. Many economic analysts predict that on a PPP basis China will soon overtake the United States as the world's largest economy. EIU, for example, projects this will occur by 2016, and that by 2030, China's economy could be 30% larger than that of the United States.[14] This would not be the first time in history that China was the world's largest economy (see text box).

The Decline and Rise of China's Economy

According to a study by economist Angus Maddison, China was the world's largest economy in 1820, accounting for an estimated 32.9% of global GDP. However, foreign and civil wars, internal strife, weak and ineffective governments, natural disasters (some of which were man-made), and distortive economic policies caused China's share of global GDP on a PPP basis to shrink significantly. By 1952, China's share of global GDP had fallen to 5.2%, and by 1978, it slid to 4.9%.[15] The adoption of economic reforms by China in the late 1970s led to a surge in China's economic growth and has helped restore China as a major global economic power.

Source: The Organization for Economic Cooperation and Development, *Chinese Economic Performance in the Long Run, 960-2030*, by Angus Maddison, 2007.

The PPP measurement also raises China's 2011 per capita GDP (from $5,460) to $8,650, which was 17.9% of the U.S. level. The EIU projects this level will rise to 34.3% by 2030. Thus, although China will likely become the world's largest economy in a few years on a PPP basis, it will likely take many years for its living standards to approach U.S. levels.[16]

Table 2. Comparisons of Chinese, Japanese, and U.S. GDP and Per Capita GDP in Nominal U.S. Dollars and a Purchasing Power Parity Basis: 2011

	China	Japan	United States
Nominal GDP ($ billions)	7,208	5,871	15,094
GDP in PPP ($ billions)	11,425	4,384	15,094
Nominal Per Capita GDP ($)	5,460	46,420	48,410
Per Capita GDP in PPP ($)	8,650	34,660	48,410

Source: Economist Intelligence Unit estimates using World Bank PPP data.

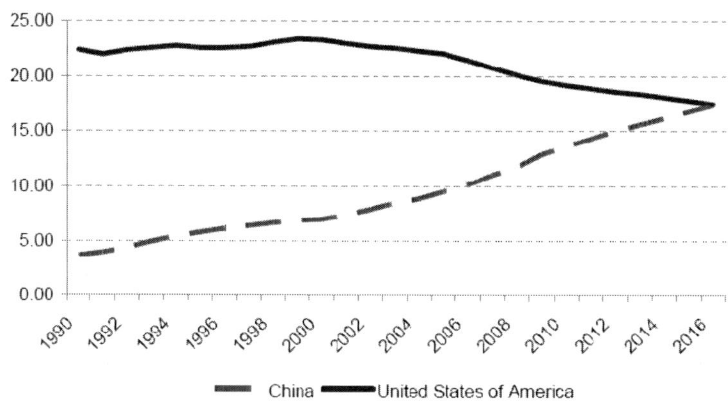

Source: Economist Intelligence Unit.
Note: Based on estimates of GDP on a PPP basis.

Figure 4. Chinese and U.S. GDP as a Percent of Global Total: 1990-2011 and Projections through 2016; (percent).

FOREIGN DIRECT INVESTMENT (FDI) IN CHINA

China's trade and investment reforms and incentives led to a surge in FDI beginning in the early 1990s.

Such flows have been a major source of China's productivity gains and rapid economic and trade growth. There were reportedly 445,244 foreign-invested enterprises (FIEs) registered in China in 2010, employing 55.2 million workers or 15.9% of the urban workforce.[17]

As indicated in Figure 5, FIEs account for a significant share of China's industrial output. That level rose from 2.3% in 1990 to a high of 35.9% in 2003, but fell to 27.1% by 2010.[18]

In addition, FIE's are responsible for a significant level of China's foreign trade. In 2011, FIEs in China accounted for 52.4% of China's exports and 49.6% of its imports, although this level was down from its peak in 2006 when FIEs' share of Chinese exports and imports was 58.2% and 59.7%, respectively, as indicated in Figure 6. FIEs in China dominate China's high technology exports.

From 2002 to 2010, the share of China's high tech exports by FIEs rose from 79% to 82%. During the same period, the share of China's high tech exports by wholly owned foreign firms (which excludes foreign joint ventures with Chinese firms) rose from 55% to 67%.

Source: Invest in China (www.fdi.gov.cn)

Figure 5. Industrial Output by Foreign-Invested Firms in China as a Share of National Total: 1990-2010; (percent).

According to the Chinese government, annual FDI inflows into China grew from $2 billion in 1985 to $108 billion in 2008. Due to the effects of the global economic slowdown, FDI flows to China fell by 12.2% to $90 billion in

2009. They totaled $106 billion in 2010 and $116 billion in 2011 (see Figure 7). Chinese data for January-October 2012 indicate that FDI fell by 3.5%% on a year-on-year basis; FDI into China will likely total around $112.1 billion for the full year.

Hong Kong was reported as the largest source of FDI flows to China in 2011 (63.9% of total), followed by Taiwan, Japan, Singapore, and the United States.

The cumulative level (or stock) of FDI in China at the end of 2011 is estimated at $1.2 trillion, making it one of the world's largest destinations of FDI. According to the United Nations Conference on Trade and Development, China was the world's second-largest destination for FDI flows in 2011, after the United States (see Figure 8).

The largest sources of cumulative FDI in China for 1979-2011 were Hong Kong (43.5% of total), the British Virgin Islands, Japan, the United States, and Taiwan (see Table 3).[19]

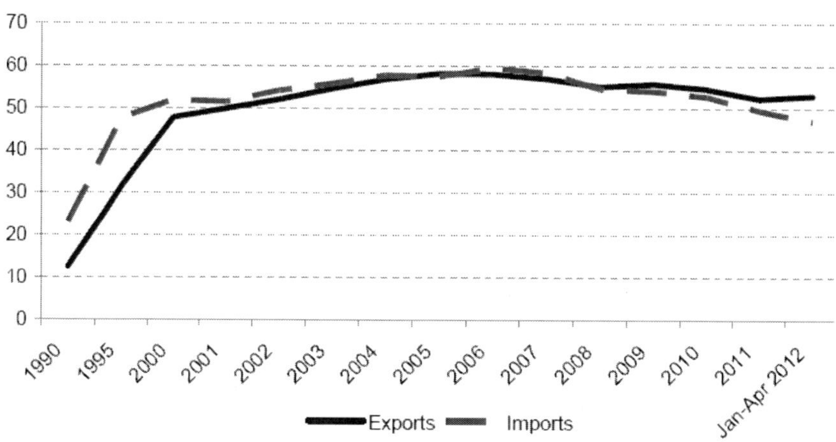

Source: "Invest in China (http://www.fdi.gov.cn/pub/FDI Note: Data for 2012 are January-April 2012.

Figure 6. Share of China's Exports and Imports Attributed to Foreign-Invested Enterprises in China: 1990-2012*; (percent).

According to Chinese data, annual U.S. FDI flows to China peaked at $5.4 billion in 2002 (10.2% of total FDI in China). In 2011, they were $3.0 billion or 2.6% of total FDI (see Figure 9).[20] From January to October 2012, U.S. FDI in China rose by 3.8% (year-on-year).

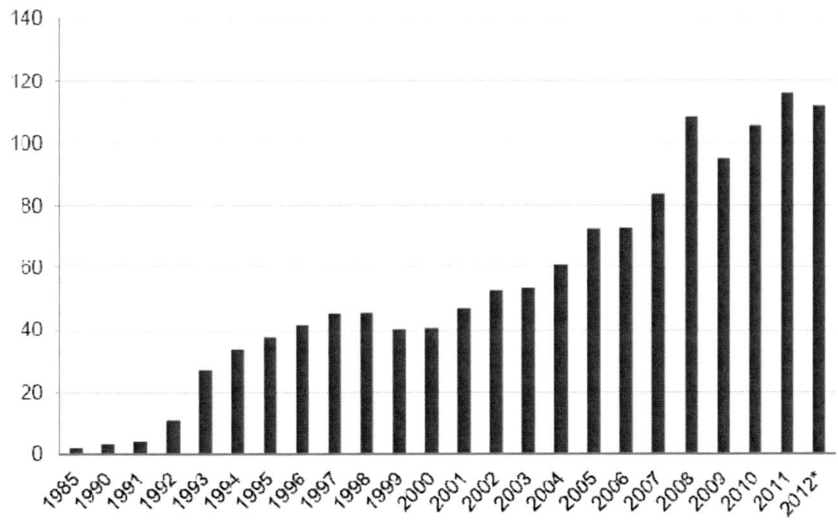

Source: United Nations Conference on Trade and Investment and Invest China.
Note: Data for 2012 are estimated, based on actual data for January-October 2012.

Figure 7. Annual FDI Flows to China: 1985-2011and estimate for 2012; ($ billions).

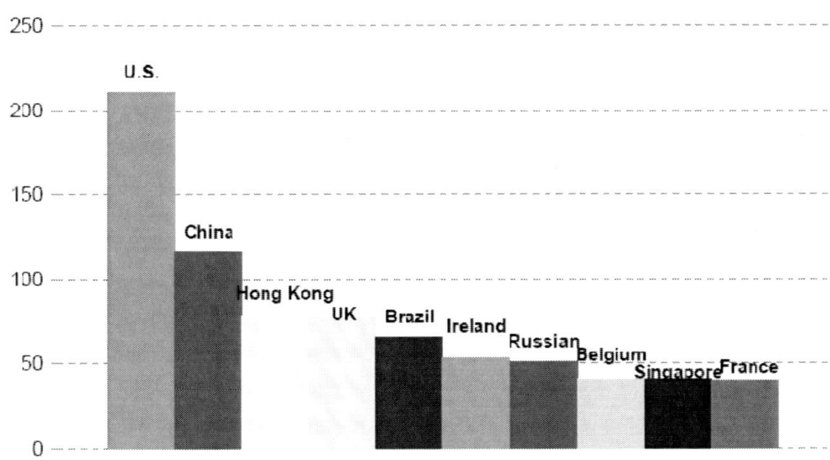

Source: United Nations Conference on Trade and Investment and Invest and Chinese Ministry of Commerce.
Note: Data for China are official Chinese data; all are estimates by the United Nations.

Figure 8. Major Recipients of Global FDI Inflows in 2011; ($ billions).

Table 3. Major Sources of FDI in China: 1979-2011 ($ billions and % of total)

	Estimated Cumulative Utilized FDI: 1979-2011		Utilized FDI in 2011	
Country	Amount	% of Total	Amount	% of Total
Total	1,224.0	100.0	116.1	100.0
Hong Kong	533.2	43.5	77.0	66.3
British Virgin Islands*	111.8	9.1	NA	NA
Japan	79.9	6.5	6.3	5.4
United States	68.1	5.6	3.0	2.6
Taiwan	58.7	4.8	6.7	5.8
Singapore	53.4	4.5	6.3	5.4
South Korea	49.9	4.1	2.6	2.2

Source: Chinese Ministry of Commerce and Chinese Statistical Yearbook.

Note: Ranked by cumulative top seven sources of FDI in China through 2011. *Data for the British Virgin Islands are through 2010.

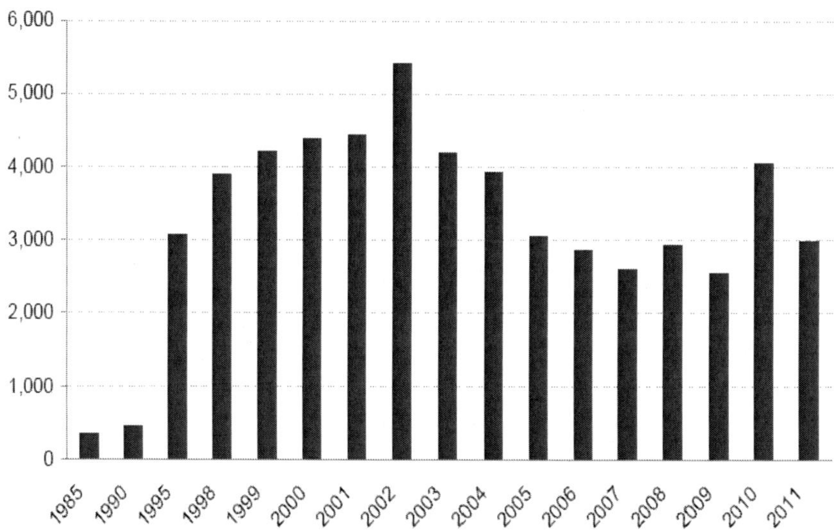

Source: Chinese Ministry of Commerce and Chinese Yearbook, various years.

Note: Chinese and U.S. data on bilateral FDI flows differ sharply because of different methodologies used.

Figure 9. Annual U.S. FDI Flows to China: 1985-2011; ($ millions).

China's Growing FDI Outflows

A key aspect of China's economic modernization and growth strategy during the 1980s and 1990s was to attract FDI into China to help boost the development of domestic firms. Investment by Chinese firms abroad was sharply restricted. However, in 2000, China's leaders initiated a new "go global" strategy, which sought to encourage Chinese firms (primarily SOEs) to invest overseas. One key factor driving this investment is China's massive accumulation of foreign exchange reserves. Traditionally, a significant level of those reserves has been invested in relatively safe, but low-yielding, assets, such as U.S. Treasury securities. On September 29, 2007, the Chinese government officially launched the China Investment Corporation (CIC) in an effort to seek more profitable returns on its foreign exchange reserves and diversify away from its U.S. dollar holdings. The CIC was originally funded at $200 billion, making it one of the world's largest sovereign wealth funds.[21] Another factor behind the government's drive to encourage more outward FDI flows has been to obtain natural resources, such as oil and minerals, deemed by the government as necessary to sustain China's rapid economic growth.[22] In June 2005, the China National Offshore Oil Corporation (CNOOC), through its Hong Kong subsidiary (CNOOC Ltd.), made a bid to buy a U.S. energy company, UNOCAL, for $18.5 billion, although CNOOC later withdrew its bid due to opposition by several congressional Members. Finally, the Chinese government has indicated its goal of developing globally competitive Chinese firms with their own brands. Investing in foreign firms, or acquiring them, is viewed as a method for Chinese firms to obtain technology, management skills, and often, internationally recognized brands, needed to help Chinese firms become more globally competitive. For example, in April 2005 Lenovo Group Limited, a Chinese computer company, purchased IBM Corporation's personal computer division for $1.75 billion.[23] Similarly, overseas FDI in new plants and businesses is viewed as developing multinational Chinese firms with production facilities and R&D operations around the world.

China has become a significant source of global FDI outflows, which rose from $2.7 billion in 2002 to $67.6 billion in 2011 (see Figure 10). In 2011, China ranked as the ninth-largest source of global FDI, according to the United Nations (see Figure 11).[24] The stock of China's outward FDI through 2011 is estimated at $384.9 billion.

China's data indicate that the top five destinations of its FDI outflows in 2010 were Hong Kong (which accounted for 56.5% of total), the British Virgin Islands, the Cayman Islands, Luxembourg, and Australia (the United

States ranked seventh). In terms of the stock of Chinese FDI outflows, the largest destinations were Hong Kong (62.8% of total), the British Virgin Islands, the Cayman Islands, Australia, and Singapore (the United States ranked seventh).[25] According to China's Ministry of Commerce, 4 out of 10 of the biggest overseas Chinese corporate investors were oil companies (based on FDI stock through 2010).[26]

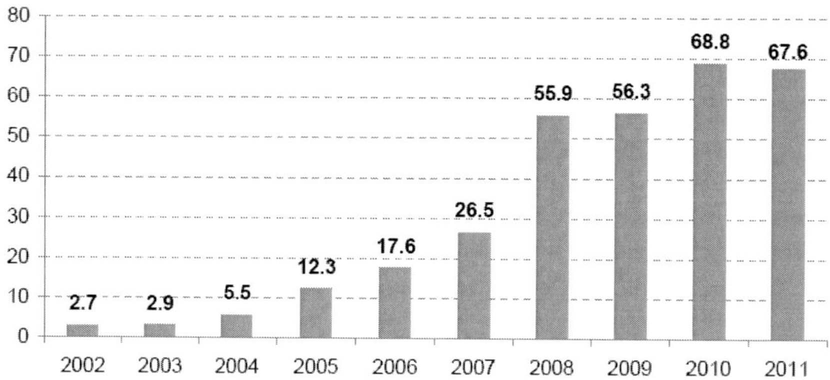

Source: Ministry of Commerce, 2011 Statistical Bulletin of China's Outward Foreign Direct Investment, 2011. Data for 2011 are from the United Nations.

Figure 10. China's Annual FDI Outflows: 2002-2011; ($ billions).

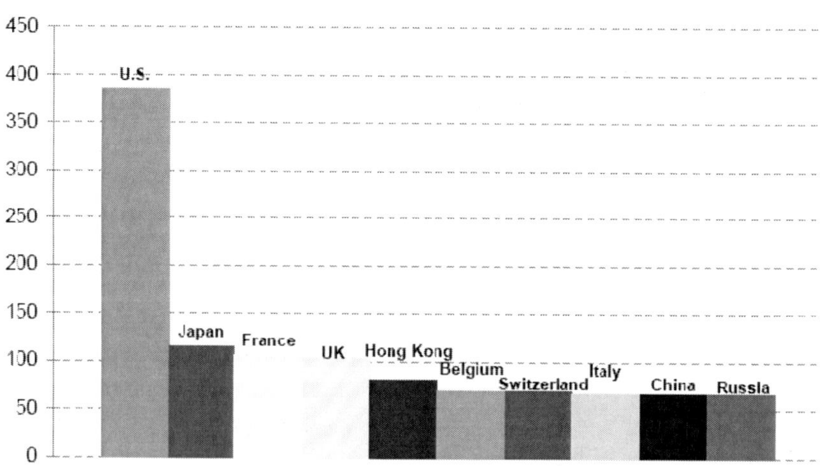

Source: United Nations estimates.

Figure 11. Major Sources of Global FDI Outflows in 2011; $billions.

According to A Capital Dragon Index, a firm that tracks China's FDI, 56% of China's outbound FDI in 2011 was in greenfield projects (such as new plants and business facilities) and 44% involved mergers and acquisitions. In terms of sectors, 51% of China's 2011 FDI went to resources (such as oil and minerals), 22% to chemicals, 14% to services, 12% to industry, and 1% to automotive. SOEs accounted for 72% of Chinese FDI that involved mergers and acquisitions in 2011.[27] A Capital Dragon Index estimates that China's first quarter 2012 outbound FDI was $21.4 billion and that SOEs accounted for 98% of mergers and acquisitions, which were largely in resources.[28]

CHINA'S MERCHANDISE TRADE PATTERNS

Economic reforms and trade and investment liberalization have helped transform China into a major trading power. Chinese merchandise exports rose from $14 billion in 1979 to $1.9 trillion in 2011, while merchandise imports over this period grew from $16 billion to $1.7 trillion (see Table 4 and Figure 12). From 1990 to 2011, the annual growth of China's exports and imports averaged 19.5% and 18.4%, respectively (see Figure 13).

Although Chinese exports and imports dropped sharply in 2009 (over 2008 levels) because of the global economic slowdown, they both recovered in 2010 and exceeded pre-crisis levels. In 2011, China's exports and imports rose by 20.3% and 24.9%, respectively. However, from January to October 2012, China's exports and imports grew by only 7.4% and 5.o%, respectively, over the same period in 2011. China's merchandise trade surplus grew sharply from 2004 to 2008, but fell sharply in 2009-2011. China's merchandise trade surplus fell from its peak of $297.4 billion in 2007 to $157.9 billion—a 46.9% decline. Based on January-October 2012 trade data, China's trade surplus for the full year could increase to about $212.5 billion.

China overtook Germany in 2009 to become the world's largest merchandise exporter and the second-largest importer (see Figure 14 and Figure 15). As indicated in Figure 16, China's share of global exports nearly tripled from 2000 to 2012, rising from 3.9% to 11.5% 2000 to 10.4% in 2011;[29] the World Bank projects this figure could increase to 20% by 2030.[30] Merchandise trade surpluses, large-scale foreign investment, and large purchases of foreign currencies to maintain its exchange rate with the dollar and other currencies have enabled China to become by far the world's largest holder of foreign exchange reserves at $3.29 trillion at the end of September 2012.

Table 4. China's Merchandise World Trade: 1979-2011 and 2012 Estimates ($ billions)

Year	Exports	Imports	Trade Balance
1979	13.7	15.7	–2.0
1980	18.1	19.5	–1.4
1985	27.3	42.5	–15.3
1990	62.9	53.9	9.0
1995	148.8	132.1	16.7
2000	249.2	225.1	24.1
2001	266.2	243.6	22.6
2002	325.6	295.2	30.4
2003	438.4	412.8	25.6
2004	593.4	561.4	32.0
2005	762.0	660.1	101.9
2006	969.1	791.5	177.6
2007	1,218.0	955.8	262.2
2008	1,428.9	1,131.5	297.4
2009	1,202.0	1,003.9	198.2
2010	1,578.4	1,393.9	184.5
2011	1,899.3	1,741.4	157.9
2012 estimate	2,040.2	1,827.7	212.5

Source: Global Trade Atlas.

Note: Data for 2012 are estimates using actual data for January-October 2012.

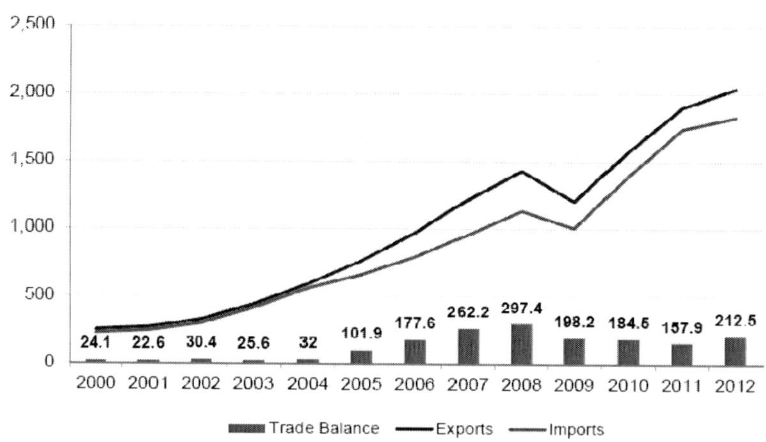

Source: Economist Intelligence Unit.

Note: Data for 2012 are estimates based on actual data for January-October 2012.

Figure 12. China's Merchandise Trade: 2000-2011 and 2012 Estimates; ($ billions).

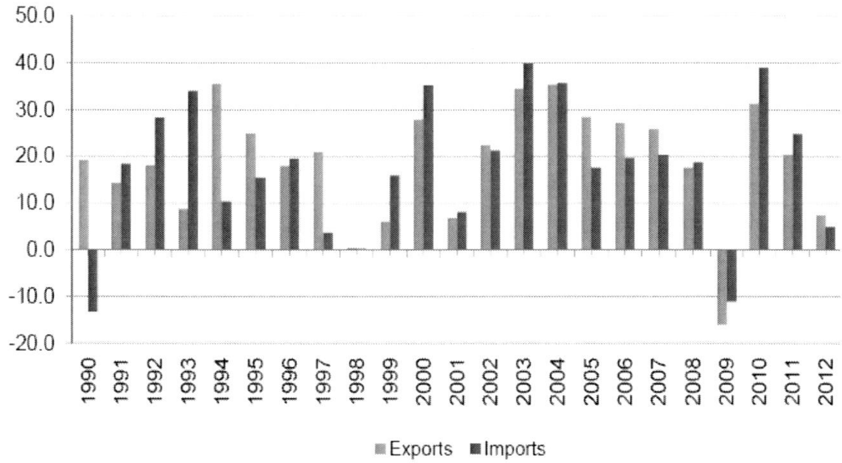

Source: Global Trade Atlas using official Chinese data.

Note: Data for 2012 are estimates based on actual data for January-October 2012.

Figure 13. Annual Change in China's Merchandise Exports and Imports: 1990-2011 and 2012 Estimates; (percent).

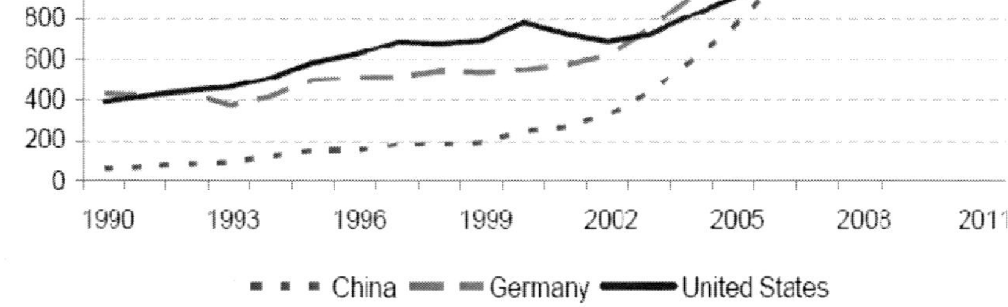

Source: Economist Intelligence Unit.

Note: Top three global importers in 2011.

Figure 14. Merchandise Exports by China, Germany and the United States: 1990-2011; ($ billions).

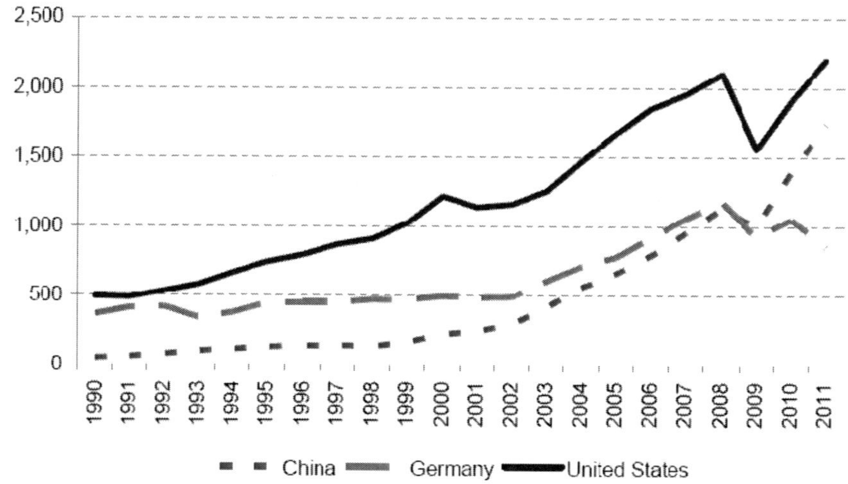

Source: Economist Intelligence Unit.
Note: Top three global importers in 2011.

Figure 15. Merchandise Imports by China, Germany, and the United States: 1990-2011; ($ billions).

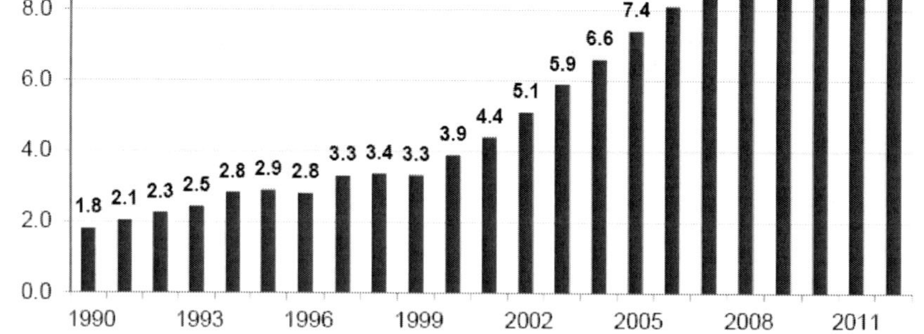

Source: Economist Intelligence Unit.
Note: Data for 2012 is estimated.

Figure 16. China's Global Share of Merchandise Exports: 1990-2011and 2012 Estimate; ($ billions).

China's Major Trading Partners

Table 5 lists Chinese trade data on its major trading partners in 2011, which included the 27 countries that make up the European Union (EU27), the United States, Japan, and the 10 nations that constitute the Association of Southeast Asian Nations (ASEAN).[31] China's largest export markets were the EU27, the United States, Hong Kong, and ASEAN, while its top sources for imports were the EU27, Japan, ASEAN, and South Korea. According to Chinese data, it maintained substantial trade surpluses with the United States, the EU27, and Hong Kong, but reported large deficits with Taiwan, South Korea, and Japan. China reported that it had a $206.2 billion trade surplus with the United States, but U.S. data show that it had a $295.5 billion deficit with China. These trade imbalance data disparities occur with many of China's other major trading partners as well. China reported that it had a $46.7 billion trade deficit with Japan, while Japan reported that it had a $22.1 billion trade deficit with China. These differences appear to be largely caused by how China's trade via Hong Kong is counted in official trade data. China treats a large share of its exports through Hong Kong as Chinese exports to Hong Kong for statistical purposes, while many countries that import Chinese products through Hong Kong generally attribute their origin to China for statistical purposes, including the United States.[32]

Table 5. China's Major Trading Partners in 2011 ($ billions)

Country	Total Trade	Chinese Exports	Chinese Imports	China's Trade Balance	Foreign Partner's Reported Trade Balance with China
European Union	567.2	356.0	211.2	144.8	-217.6
United States	442.4	324.3	118.1	206.2	-295.5
Japan	342.1	147.7	194.4	-46.7	-22.1
ASEAN	362.4	169.9	192.5	-22.6	NA
Hong Kong	277.9	267.5	10.4	257.1	26.6
South Korea	250.6	82.9	167.7	-84.8	47.8
Taiwan	155.0	30.1	124.9	-94.8	34.7
Total Chinese Trade	3,640.7	1,899.3	1,741.4	157.9	--

Source: Global Trade Atlas and World Trade Atlas.

Note: Rankings according to China's total trade in 2011.

Major Chinese Trade Commodities

China's abundance of low-cost labor has made it internationally competitive in many low-cost, labor-intensive manufactures. The average hourly labor cost for manufacturing in China in 2010 (at $2) was 5.7% the cost in the United States (at $35).[33] As a result, manufactured products constitute a significant share of China's trade. A substantial amount of China's imports is comprised of parts and components that are assembled into finished products, such as consumer electronic products and computers, and then exported. Often, the value-added to such products in China by Chinese workers is relatively small compared to the total value of the product when it is shipped abroad. China's top 10 exports and imports in 2011 are listed in Table 6 and Table 7, respectively, using the harmonized tariff system (HTS) on a two-digit level. Major exports included electrical machinery (such as computers and parts), machinery, knit apparel, and woven apparel, while major imports included electrical machinery, mineral fuel, machinery, and ores.

Table 6. Major Chinese Exports: 2011

HS Code	Description	$billions	Percent of Total	2011/2010 % Change
	World	1,899.3	100	20.3
85	Electrical machinery (such as computers and parts)	445.8	23.5	14.6
84	Machinery	353.9	18.6	14.2
61	Knit apparel	80.2	4.2	20.2
62	Woven apparel	63.1	3.3	16.0
90	Optical, photographic, cinematographic, measuring checking, precision, medical or surgical instruments and apparatus; parts and accessories thereof	60.7	3.2	16.5
94	Furniture and bedding	59.4	3.1	17.3
73	Iron and steel products	51.2	2.7	30.8
87	Vehicles, except railway (mainly auto parts, motorcycles, trucks, and bicycles)	49.6	2.6	29.2
39	Plastic	45.5	2.4	30.9
89	Ships and boats	43.7	2.3	8.5

Source: *World Trade Atlas*, using official Chinese statistics.

Notes: Top 10 exports in 2011, 2-digit level, harmonized tariff system.

Table 7. Major Chinese Imports: 2011

HS Code	Description	$ billions	Percent of Total	2011/2010 % change
	World	1,741.4	100	24.9
85	Electrical machinery	351.0	20.2	11.6
27	Mineral fuel, oil etc.	273.5	15.7	45.2
84	Machinery	199.6	11.5	15.8
26	Ores, slag, and ash	150.7	8.7	39.5
90	Optical, photographic, cinematographic, measuring, checking, precision, medical or surgical instruments	99.0	5.7	10.4
	and apparatus; parts and accessories thereof			
39	Plastic	70.2	4.0	10.2
87	Vehicles, not railway (mainly autos and parts)	65.3	3.8	32.2
29	Organic chemicals	63.2	3.6	31.0
74	Copper and articles thereof	54.3	3.1	18.0
98	Special Classification	49.5	2.8	168.5

Source: *World Trade Atlas*, using official Chinese statistics.
Notes: Top 10 imports in 2011, two-digit level, harmonized tariff schedule.

China's Growing Appetite for Energy

China's rapid economic growth has fueled a growing demand for energy, such as petroleum and coal, and that demand is becoming an increasingly important factor in determining global energy prices. According to the International Energy Agency (IEA), China overtook the United States in 2009 as the world's largest energy user (in comparison, China's energy use was only half that of that of the United States in 2000). According to IEA projections, China's demand for energy from 2008 (the baseline year) to 2035 will account for 30% of the projected increase in global demand for energy during this period. By 2035, China is projected to consume 70% more energy than the United States (even though, on a per capita basis, China's energy consumption will be less than half of U.S. levels).[34]

China is the world's second-largest consumer of oil products (after the United States) at 9.8 million barrels per day (bpd) in 2011 (compared to 3.9

million in 1997), and that level rises to 16.9 million bpd by 2035.[35] China became a net oil importer (i.e., imports minus exports) in 1993. Net oil imports grew from 632,000 bpd in 1997 to about 5.0 million bpd in 2010 (see Figure 17), making it the world's second-largest net oil importer after the United States.[36] China's net oil imports are projected to rise to 13.1 million bpd by 2030, a level that would be comparable to the European Union in that year.[37]

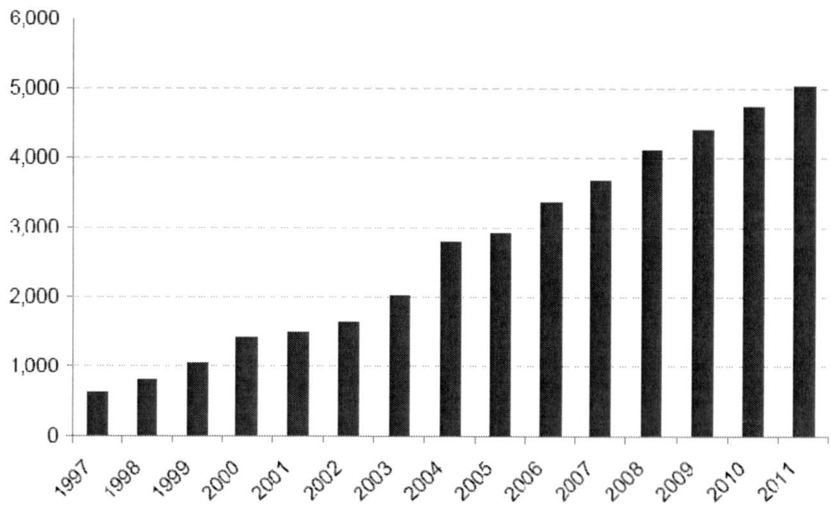

Source: U.S. Energy Administration, China Energy Newswire, and British Petroleum June 2010 Statistical Review of World Energy. Data for 2010 and 2011 from China Daily.

Figure 17. China's Net Oil Imports: 1997-2011; (Thousands BPD).

China's Regional and Bilateral Free Trade Agreements

The Chinese government has maintained an active policy of boosting trade and investment ties around the world, especially with countries in Asia. To that end, China has entered into a number of regional and bilateral trade agreements, or is in the process of doing so. China currently has free trade agreements (FTAs) with ASEAN, Pakistan, Chile, Hong Kong, Macau, New Zealand, Singapore, Pakistan, Peru, and Costa Rica. China also has an economic cooperation framework agreement (ECFA) with Taiwan. China is currently in the process of negotiating FTAs with the Cooperation Council for the Arab States of the Gulf (which includes Saudi Arabia, Kuwait, the United

Arab Emirates, Qatar, and Bahrain), Australia, Iceland, Norway, Switzerland, and the Southern African Customs Union (which includes South Africa, Botswana, Lesotho, Namibia, and Swaziland). In May 2012, China, Japan, and South Korea agreed to begin negotiations for an FTA in 2012. China has also considered negotiating an FTA with India, but with little progress to date.[38]

Major Long-Term Challenges Facing the Chinese Economy

China's economy has shown remarkable growth over the past several years, and many economists project that it will enjoy fairly healthy growth in the near future. However, economists caution that these projections are likely to occur only if China continues to make major reforms to its economy. Failure to implement such reforms could endanger future growth. They note that China's current economic model has resulted in a number of negative economic (and social) outcomes, such as over-reliance on fixed investment and exporting for its economic growth, extensive inefficiencies that exist in many sectors (due largely to government industrial policies), wide-spread pollution, and growing income inequality, to name a few. Many of China's economic problems and challenges stem from its incomplete transition to a free market economy and from imbalances that have resulted from the government's goal of economic growth at all costs.

China's Incomplete Transition to a Market Economy

Despite China's three-decade history of widespread economic reforms, Chinese officials contend that China is a "socialist-market economy." This appears to indicate that the government accepts and allows the use of free market forces in a number of areas to help grow the economy, but where the government still plays a major role in the country's economic development.

Industrial Policies and SOEs

According to the World Bank, "China has become one of the world's most active users of industrial policies and administrations."[39] According to one estimate, China's SOEs may account for up of 50% of non-agriculture GDP.[40] In addition, although the number of SOEs has declined sharply, they continue to dominate a number of sectors (such as petroleum and mining, telecommunications, utilities, transportation, and various industrial sectors);

are shielded from competition; are the main sectors encouraged to invest overseas; and dominate the listings on China's stock indexes.[41] One study found that SOEs constituted 50% of the 500 largest manufacturing companies in China and 61% of the top 500 service sector enterprises.[42] It is estimated that there were 154,000 SOEs as of 2008, and while these accounted for only 3.1% of all enterprises in China, they held 30% of the value of corporate assets in the manufacturing and services sectors.[43] Of the 58 Chinese firms on the 2011 *Fortune* Global 500 list, 54 were identified as having government ownership of 50% or more.[44] The World Bank estimates that more than one in four SOEs lose money.[45]

The Banking System

China's banking system is largely controlled by the central government, which attempts to ensure that capital (credit) flows to industries deemed by the government to be essential to China's economic development. SOEs are believed to receive preferential credit treatment by government banks, while private firms must often pay higher interest rates or obtain credit elsewhere. According to one estimate, SOEs accounted for 85% ($1.4 trillion) of all bank loans in 2009.[46] In addition, the government sets interest rates for depositors at very low rates, often below the rate of inflation, which keeps the price of capital relatively low for firms.[47] It is believed that oftentimes SOEs do not repay their loans, which may have saddled the banks with a large amount of non-performing loans. In addition, local governments are believed to have borrowed extensively from state banks shortly after the global economic slowdown began to impact the Chinese economy to fund infrastructure and other initiatives. Some contend these measures could further add to the amount of non-performing loans held by the banks. Many analysts contend that one of the biggest weaknesses of the banking system is that it lacks the ability to ration and allocate credit according to market principles, such as risk assessment.

An Undervalued Currency

China does not allow its currency to float and therefore must make large-scale purchases of dollars to keep the exchange rate within certain target levels. Although the renminbi (RMB) has appreciated against the dollar in real terms by about 40% since reforms were introduced in July 2005, analysts contend that it remains highly undervalued.[48] China's undervalued currency makes its exports less expensive, and its imports more expensive, than would occur under a floating exchange rate system. In order to maintain its exchange rate target, the government must purchase foreign currency (such as the dollar) by expanding the money supply. This makes it much more difficult for the government to use monetary policy to combat inflation.[49]

Many economists argue that China's industrial policies have sharply limited competition and the growth of the private sector, caused over-capacity in many industries, and distorted markets by artificially lowering the costs of various factor costs (such as capital, water, land, and energy) below market levels in order to promote targeted industrial sectors. Such policies have come at the expense of other (non-industrial) sectors of the economy, such as services.

Implications of China's "Unbalanced" Economic Growth Model

China's economic model, until recently, has emphasized rapid economic growth above nearly all other considerations. Various data show that, while China's GDP has risen rapidly over the past 33 years, Chinese households do not appear to have shared equally in that growth. In addition, China's economic model has resulted in a number of significant problems that may negatively affect future growth.

Overdependence on Exporting and Fixed Investment

The IMF estimates that fixed investment related to tradable goods plus net exports together accounted for over 60% of China's GDP growth from 2001 to 2008 (up from 40% from 1990 to 2000), which was significantly higher than in the G-7 countries (16%), the euro area (30%), and the rest of Asia (35%). China's fixed investment as a percentage of GDP is the highest of any major economy and its importance has been growing. As shown in Figure 18, fixed investment as a percent of GDP increased from 25% in 1990 to 48.5% in 2011. On the other hand, during the same period, private consumption as a percent of GDP fell from 48.8% to 33.9%.[50] China's private consumption as a share of GDP is the lowest of any major economy.[51] In addition, as indicated in Figure 19, personal disposable income in China as a share of GDP has also been falling over the past decade or so, from 47.6% in 2000 to 42.2% in 2011.[52] China's overall savings rate as a percent of GDP in 2011 was 52.1%, which was the highest rate of any major economy.

Many economists contend that the falling share of private consumption and disposable income relative to GDP is largely caused by two main factors: China's banking policies and the lack of an adequate social safety net. The

Chinese government places restrictions on the export of capital. As a result, Chinese households put a large share of their savings in domestic banks. The Chinese government sets the interest rate on deposits. Often this rate is below the rate of inflation, which lowers household income. Some economists consider this policy to constitute a transfer of wealth from Chinese households to Chinese firms which benefit from low interest rates. This "tax" on household income negatively affects household consumption. Secondly, China's lack of an adequate social safety net (such as pensions, health care, unemployment insurance, and education) induces households to save a large portion of their income. According to one estimate, the average saving rate of urban households relative to their disposable incomes rose from 18% in 1995 to nearly 29% in 2009.[53] Corporations are also a major contributor to the high savings rate in China. Many Chinese firms, especially SOEs, do not pay out dividends and thus are able to retain most of their earnings. Many economists contend that requiring the SOEs to pay dividends could boost private consumption in China.

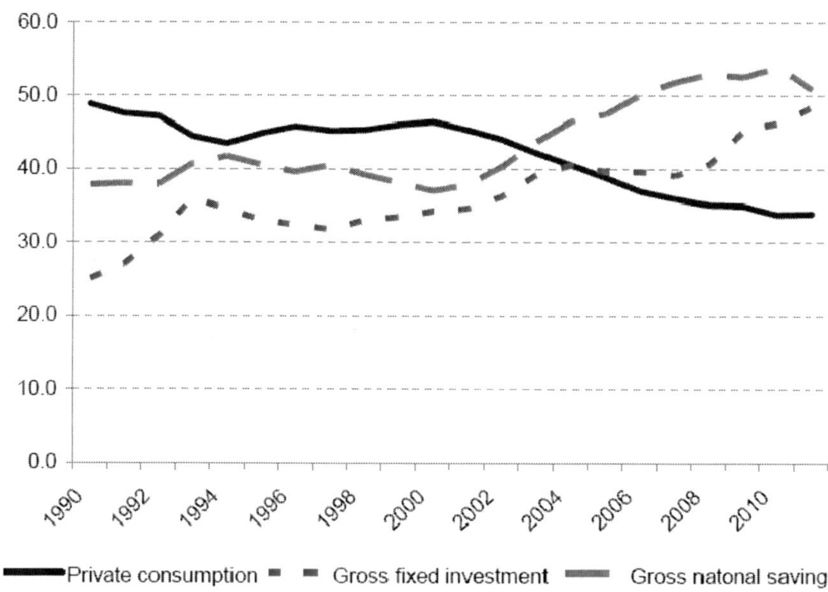

Source: Economist Intelligence Unit.

Figure 18. Chinese Gross Savings, Gross Fixed Investment, and Private Consumption as a Percent of GDP: 1990-2011; (percent).

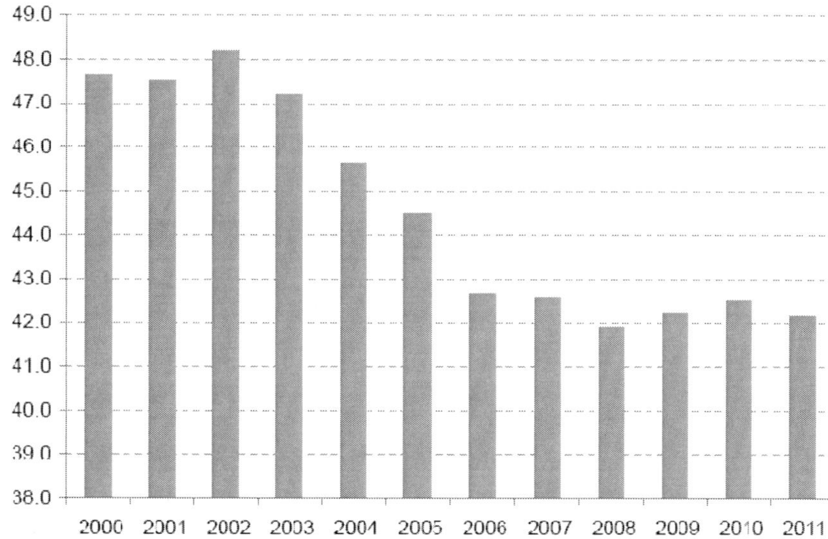

Source: Economist Intelligence Unit.

Figure 19. Chinese Disposable Personal Income as a Percent of GDP: 2000-2011; (percent).

Growing Pollution

China's economic growth model has emphasized the growth of heavy industry in China, much of which is energy-intensive and high polluting. The level of pollution in China continues to worsen, posing series health risks to the population. The Chinese government often disregards its own environmental laws in order to promote rapid economic growth. According to the World Bank, 20 out of 30 of the world's most polluted cities are in China, with significant costs to the economy (such as health problems, crop failures, and water shortages). According to one government official estimate in 2006, environmental damage costs the country $226 billion, or 10% of the country's GDP, each year.[54] The Chinese government estimated that in 2004 there were over 300 million people living in rural areas who drank unsafe water (caused by chemicals and other contaminants). Toxic spills in 2005 and 2006 threatened the water supply of millions of people. China is the largest producer and consumer of coal, which accounts for about 70% of China's energy use. In October 2009, China's media reported that thousands of children living near smelters had been found to have excessive amounts of lead in their blood. Although growing environmental degradation has been recognized as a serious problem by China's central government, it has found it difficult to induce local governments to comply with environmental laws, especially when such officials feel doing so will come at the expense of economic growth.

The EIA projects that by 2035, China's carbon dioxide emissions could be nearly double its current levels.[55] A study by ExxonMobil found that, by 2030, China's CO2 emissions could equal the level in the United States and EU combined.[56]

Other Challenges

China's economy faces a number of social and political challenges as well:

- **Public unrest.** For China's Communist Party leadership, a growing economy is its main source of political legitimacy. However, every year numerous protests occur in China over a number of issues, including pollution, government corruption, and land seizures. A number of protests in China have stemmed in part from frustrations among many Chinese (especially peasants) that they are not benefitting from China's economic reforms and rapid growth, and perceptions that those who are getting rich are doing so because they have connections with government officials. A 2005 United Nations report stated that the income gap between the urban and rural areas was among the highest in the world and warned that this gap threatens social stability. The report urged China to take greater steps to improve conditions for the rural poor, and bolster education, health care, and the social safety net.[57] It is estimated that 300 million people in China (mainly in rural areas) lacked health insurance, and many that do have basic insurance must pay a significant amount of medical expenses out of their own pocket.[58]
- **The lack of the rule of law** in China has led to widespread government corruption, financial speculation, and misallocation of investment funds. In many cases, government "connections," not market forces, are the main determinant of successful firms in China. Many U.S. firms find it difficult to do business in China because rules and regulations are generally not consistent or transparent, contracts are not easily enforced, and intellectual property rights are not protected (due to the lack of an independent judicial system). The relative lack of the rule of law and widespread government corruption in China limit competition and undermine the efficient allocation of goods and services in the economy.

- **Poor government regulatory environment**. China maintains a weak and relatively decentralized government structure to regulate economic activity in China. Laws and regulations often go unenforced or are ignored by local government officials. As a result, many firms cut corners in order to maximize profits. This has lead to a proliferation of unsafe food and consumer products being sold in China or exported abroad. Lack of government enforcement of food safety laws led to a massive recall of melamine-tainted infant milk formula that reportedly killed at least four children and sickened 53,000 others in 2008.

PLANS ANNOUNCED BY THE CHINESE GOVERNMENT TO REFORM AND RESTRUCTURE THE ECONOMY

Various government officials have publicly stated the need for China to change course from its traditional economic growth model of growth at all cost to one that balances economic growth with a number of social goals in order to develop a "socialist harmonious society," and to further modernize the economy. In March 2007, Chinese Premier Wen Jiabao stated that there are "structural problems in China's economy which cause unsteady, unbalanced, uncoordinated and unsustainable development." He defined "unsteady development" as overheated investment, excessive credit and liquidity, and merchandise trade and current account surpluses. "Unbalanced development" was described as economic disparities between rural and urban areas, regions of the country, and between economic and social development. "Uncoordinated development" was described as the lack of balance between various sectors of the economy (especially in regards to the services sector) and between investment and consumption (i.e., economic growth is mainly driven by investment and exports rather than consumer demand). Lastly, "unsustainable development" referred to problems caused by China's inefficient use of energy and resources and failure to protect the environment.

THE CENTRAL GOVERNMENT FIVE-YEAR PLANS

China's last two five-year plans (FYP), the 11th FYP (2006-2010) and the 12th FYP (2011-2015), have placed strong emphasis on promoting consumer demand, addressing income disparities (such as by boosting spending on social safety net programs), boosting energy efficiency, reducing pollution, improving the rule of law, and deepening economic reforms. Those plans have also identified a number of industries and technologies that the government has targeted for development (see text box).

China's 12th Five-Year Plan[59]

China's Five-Year Plans (FYPs) have been issued by the government since 1953. The FYP is the major vehicle for the government to establish broad economic and social goals for the time period under consideration, to coordinate investments between the central and local governments, and to oversee implementation of policy. Not only does the plan influence investments by government entities, it also provides direction for bank lending and government approvals and regulation of private and semi-private industries.

In March 2011, China's National People's Congress approved the 12th Five-Year Plan (covering the years 2011 to 2015).

The 12th FYP (2011-2015) contains three broad themes or areas of focus: (1) economic restructuring, (2) promoting greater social equality, and (3) protecting the environment. Chinese industrial policy comes into play primarily in economic restructuring but also is apparent in the other areas of focus.

Particularly noteworthy is the targeting of seven strategic emerging industries that are intended to become the backbone of China's economy in the future and to be able to compete well on a global scale.

These seven industries are (1) biotechnology, (2) new energy, (3) high-end equipment manufacturing, (4) energy conservation and environmental protection, (5) clean-energy vehicles, (6) new materials, and (7) next-generation information technology. The government reportedly intends to spend up to $2.1 trillion on these industries during the 12th FYP. Some of the highlights of the FYP include:

- achieving an average real GDP growth rate of 7% and ensuring that incomes rise at least as fast as GDP;
- consolidating inefficient sectors and promoting the services industry (with the goal of expanding service sector output to account for 47% of GDP—up four percentage points from the current level);

- promoting energy saving and new energy industries; promoting the development of nuclear, water, wind, and solar power; and expanding non-fossil fuel to account for 11.4% of primary energy consumption;
- welcoming foreign investment in modern agriculture, high-technology, and environmental protection industries;
- turning coastal regions from "world's factory" to hubs of research and development, high-end manufacturing, and services;
- lengthening high-speed railway and highway networks;
- increasing expenditure on R&D to account for 2.2% of GDP;
- expanding non-fossil fuel to account for 11.4% of primary energy consumption;
- cutting water consumption per unit of value-added industrial output by 30%, energy consumption per unit of GDP by 16%, and carbon dioxide emission per unit of GDP by 17%;
- transfer the coastal regions from the "world's factory" to hubs of R&D, high-end manufacturing, and environmental protection industries;
- increasing the minimum wage by no less than 13% on average each year; and
- building 36 million affordable apartments for low-income people.

Sources: Xinhua News Agency, Highlights of China's 12th Five-Year Plan, March 5, 2011; and APCO Worldwide, China's 12th Five-Year Plan: How it Actually Works and What's in Store For the Next Five Years, December 10, 2010.

The Drive for "Indigenous Innovation"

Many of the industrial policies that China has implemented or formulated since 2006 appear to stem largely from a comprehensive document issued by China's State Council (the highest executive organ of state power) in 1996 titled *The National Medium-and Long-Term Program for Science and Technology Development (2006-2020)*, often referred to as the MLP. The MLP appears to represent an ambitious plan to modernize the structure of China's economy by transforming it from a global center of low-tech manufacturing to a major center of innovation (by the year 2020) and a global innovation leader by 2050.

As some observers describe it, China wants to go from a model of "made in China" to "innovated in China." It also seeks to sharply reduce the country's dependence on foreign technology.

The MLP includes the stated goals of "indigenous innovation, leapfrogging in priority fields, enabling development, and leading the future."[60] Some of the broad goals of the MLP state that by 2020:

- The progress of science and technology will contribute 60% or above to China's development.
- The country's reliance on foreign technology will decline to 30% or below (from an estimated current level of 50%).
- Gross expenditures for research and development (R&D) would rise to 2.5% of gross domestic product (from 1.3% in 2005). Priority areas for increased R&D include space programs, aerospace development and manufacturing, renewable energy, computer science, and life sciences.[61]

The document states that "China must place the strengthening of indigenous innovative capability at the core of economic restructuring, growth model change, and national competitiveness enhancement.

Building an innovation-oriented country is therefore a major strategic choice for China's future development."

This goal, according to the document, is to be achieved by formulating and implementing regulations in the country's government procurement law to "encourage and protect indigenous innovation," establishing a coordination mechanism for government procurement of indigenous innovative products, requiring a first-buy policy for major domestically made high-tech equipment and products that possess proprietary intellectual property rights, providing policy support to enterprises in procuring domestic high-tech equipment, and developing "relevant technology standards" through government procurement.

CHALLENGES TO U.S. POLICY OF CHINA'S ECONOMIC RISE

China's rapid economic growth and emergence as a major economic power have given China's leadership increased confidence in its economic model. Many believe the key challenges for the United States are to convince

China that (1) it has a stake in maintaining the international trading system, which is largely responsible for its economic rise, and to take a more active leadership role in maintaining that system; and (2) that further economic and trade reforms are the surest way for China to grow and modernize its economy.

For example, by boosting domestic spending and allowing its currency to appreciate, China would import more, which would help speed economic recovery in other countries, promote more stable and balanced economic growth in China, and lessen trade protectionist pressures around the world. Lowering trade barriers on imports would boost competition in China, lower costs for consumers, and increase economic efficiency.

However, many U.S. stakeholders are concerned that China's efforts to boost the development of indigenous innovation and technology could result in greater intervention by the state (such as subsidies and trade and investment barriers), which could negatively affect U.S. IPintensive firms. Failure by China to take meaningful steps to rebalance its economy could increase tensions with its trading partners, especially if China's share of global exports continues to increase rapidly, and if that increase is viewed as being the result of non-market policies that give Chinese exports an unfair competitive advantage.[62]

Some economists contend that some economic rebalancing by China appears to have taken place in recent years, noting that China's current account surplus as a percent of GDP declined from a historical high of 10.1% in 2007 to 2.8% in 2011 (see Figure 20). However, as indicated in Figure 21, fixed investment has been the largest contributor to China's economic growth over the past five years, rather than private consumption.

Opinions differ as to the most effective way of dealing with China on major economic issues. Some support a policy of engagement with China using various forums, such as the U.S.-China Strategic and Economic Dialogue (S&ED), which holds discussions on major long-term economic issues at the highest government level. Others support a somewhat mixed policy of using engagement when possible, coupled with a more aggressive use of the World Trade Organization (WTO) dispute settlement procedures to address China's unfair trade policies. Still others, who see China as a growing threat to the U.S. economy and the global trading system, advocate a policy of trying to contain China's economic power and using punitive measures when needed to force China to "play by the rules."

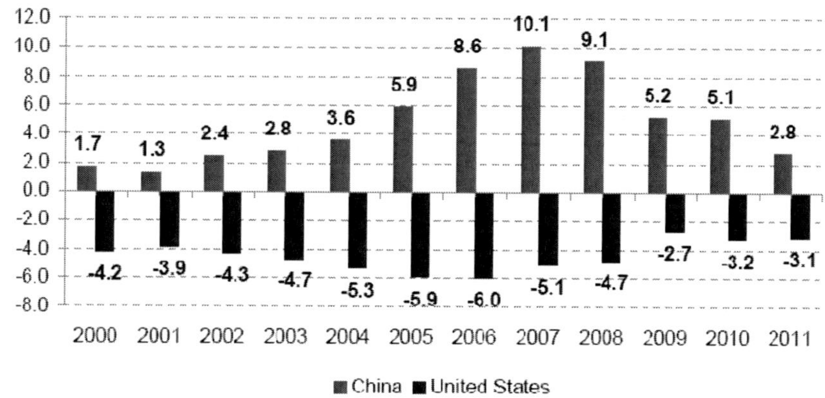

Source: International Monetary Fund.

Figure 20. Current Account Balances as a Percent of GDP for China and the United States: 2000-2011; (percent).

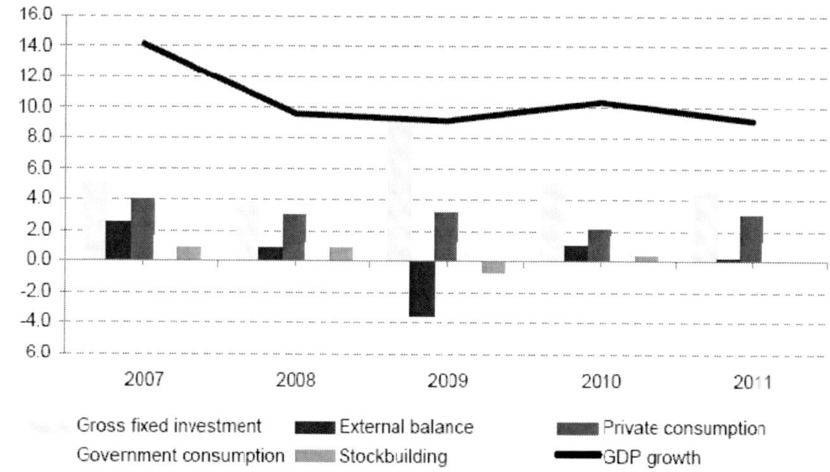

Source: Economist Intelligence Unit.

Figure 21. Sources of China's GDP Growth: 2007-2011; (% points).

China's growing economic power has made it a critical and influential player on the global stage on a number of issues important to U.S. interests, such as global economic cooperation, climate change, nuclear proliferation, and North Korean aggression.[63] China is in a position to help advance U.S. interests or to frustrate them. China's rising economy has also enabled it to boost its military capabilities, raising the prospects that China could use that power to project its interests globally, which could bring it into conflict with the United States and its allies.

U.S. policymakers face a number of complex challenges on how to deal with these issues. Can the United States compel better behavior from China via quiet diplomacy or public confrontation? Has U.S. leverage over Beijing lessened in the wake of China's economic rise, and has China's leverage over Washington increased? How will China's upcoming leadership changes affect its economic policies?" Will its new leaders promote greater economic reforms and trade liberalization or will they support greater control over the economy?[64]

End Notes

[1] The beginning of China's economic reform process began in December 1978 when the Third Plenum of the Eleventh Central Committee of the Communist Party adopted Deng Xiaoping's economic proposals. Implementation of the reforms began in 1979.

[2] Some companies use China as part of their global supply chain for manufactured parts, which are then exported and assembled elsewhere. Other firms have shifted the production of finished products from other countries (mainly in Asia) to China; they import parts and materials into China for final assembly.

[3] This reference appears to have meant that it did not matter whether an economic policy was considered to be capitalist or socialist, what really mattered was whether that policy boosted the economy.

[4] For example, China's accession to the World Trade Organization in December 2001, which required it to reduce a wide range of trade and investment barriers, helped to accelerate GDP growth and led to a sharp increase in FDI flows to China.

[5] Many analysts contend that Deng's push to implement economic reforms was largely motivated by a belief that the resulting economic growth would ensure that the Communist Party stayed in power.

[6] Chinability, *GDP Growth in China, 1952-2011*, at http://www.chinability.com/GDP.htm.

[7] During the Great Leap Forward, local Chinese officials are believed to have often exaggerated agricultural production to prove their ability to implement Mao's economic policies in order to advance their careers or to avoid getting into political trouble with Beijing. Central government officials may have also exaggerated China's economic statistics in order to illustrate the "success" of the government's economic policies.

[8] The Organization for Economic Cooperation and Development, *Chinese Economic Performance in the Long Run, 960-2030*, by Angus Maddison, 2007.

[9] Source: Economist Intelligence Unit Database.

[10] Like China, Japan experienced rapid economic growth during the early stages of its development in the post-WWII era, with real GDP averaging 11.0% from 1960-1970. However, from 1970-1980 real GDP averaged 5.4%; it was 4.1% from 1980-1990, 1.1% from 1990-2000. Japan has continued to experience relatively stagnant economic growth, in

part because of its inability to address a number of structural economic problems. See CRS Report RL30176, *Japan's "Economic Miracle": What Happened?*, by William H. Cooper

[11] Note, long-term economic projections should be viewed with caution.

[12] On a nominal dollar basis, China overtook Japan in 2010 to become the world's second largest economy (after the United States).

[13] In other words, the PPP data reflect what the value of China's goods and services would be if they were sold in the United States.

[14] However, such long-term economic projections should be viewed with caution.

[15] In comparison, the U.S. share of global GDP rose from 1.8% in 1820 to 27.5% in 1952, but declined to 21.6% by 1978.

[16] EIU database, surveyed on May 22, 2012.

[17] China 2011 Statistical Yearbook.

[18] Industrial output is defined by the Chinese government as the total volume of final industrial products produced and industrial services provided during a given period. Source: China 2011 Statistical Yearbook.

[19] Much of the FDI originating from the British Virgin Islands and Hong Kong may originate from other foreign investors. In addition, some Chinese investors might be using these locations to shift funds overseas in order to reinvest in China to take advantage of preferential investment policies (this practice is often referred to as "round-tipping"). Thus, the actual level of FDI in China may be overstated.

[20] U.S. data on bilateral FDI flows with China differ significantly with Chinese data. For additional info on bilateral FDI flows based on U.S. data, see CRS Report RL33536, *China-U.S. Trade Issues*, by Wayne M. Morrison.

[21] See, CRS Report RL34337, *China's Sovereign Wealth Fund*, by Michael F. Martin.

[22] Chinese oil and mineral companies are dominated by SOEs.

[23] The Chinese government is believed to be Lenovo's largest shareholder.

[24] United Nations Conference on Trade and Development, Global Investment Trade Monitor, April 12, 2012.

[25] It is likely that a significant level of Chinese FDI in the British Virgin Islands, the Cayman Islands, and Hong Kong are re-directed elsewhere.

[26] Chinese Ministry of Commerce, *2010 Statistical Bulletin of China's Outward Foreign Direct Investment*, October 2011.

[27] A Capital Dragon Index, *2011 Full Year*, available at http://www.acapital.hk /dragonindex /datasheets.

[28] A Capital Dragon Index, *2012 Q1*, available at http://www.acapital.hk /dragonindex /datasheets.

[29] Economist Intelligence Unit, *Data Tools*.

[30] The World Bank, China 2030, *Building a Modern, Harmonious, and Creative High-Income Society*, 2012, p. 14. Hereafter referred to as World Bank, China 2030.

[31] ASEAN members include Brunei, Cambodia, Indonesia, Laos, Malaysia, Myanmar (Burma), the Philippines, Singapore, Thailand, and Vietnam.

[32] See CRS Report RS22640, *What's the Difference?—Comparing U.S. and Chinese Trade Data*, by Michael F. Martin.

[33] In addition, the overall average monthly wage in China, at $539 (nominal U.S. dollars) in 2011, was about 13% U.S. levels (although the disparity would lessen if purchasing power data were used). Source: Economist Intelligence Unit data tool.

[34] International Energy Agency, *2011 World Energy Outlook*, November 2011, available at http://www.iea.org/weo.

[35] U.S. Energy Information Administration, *Forecasts and Analysis*, at http://www.eia.doe.gov /oiaf/forecasting

[36] China overtook Japan as the second largest net oil importer in 2009.

[37] EIA, *International Energy Outlook*, September 19, 2011, available at http://www.eia.gov /forecasts/ieo.

[38] Chinese Ministry of Commerce, *China FTA Network*, available at http://fta.mofcom.gov.cn /english/fta_qianshu.shtml.

[39] The World Bank, *China:2030*, p. 114.

[40] U.S.-China Economic and Security Review Commission, An Analysis of State-owned Enterprises and State Capitalism in China, by Andrew Szamosszegi and Cole Kyle, October 26, 2011, p.1.

[41] The nature of China's SOEs has become increasing complex. Many SOEs appear to be run like private companies. For example, and a number of SOEs have made initial public offerings in China's stock markets and those in other countries (including the United States), although the Chinese government is usually the largest shareholder. It is not clear to what extent the Chinese government attempts to influence decisions made by the SOE's which have become shareholding companies.

[42] Xiao Geng, Xiuke Yang, and Anna Janus, *State-owned Enterprises in China, Reform Dynamics and Impacts*, 2009, p.155.

[43] The World Bank, *State-Owned Enterprises in China: How Big Are They?,* January 19, 2010.

[44] Global 500, The World's Largest Corporations," *Fortune*, July 25, 2011, available at http://money.cnn.com/magazines

[45] World Bank, *China 2030*, p.25.

[46] The Economist, *State Capitalism's Global Reach, New Masters of the Universe, How State Enterprise is Spreading*, January 21, 2012, available at http://www.economist.com /node/21542925.

[47] Some economists argue that a significant portion of China's SOEs could not stay in business if they had to pay a market-based interest rate for credit.

[48] See CRS Report RS21625, *China's Currency Policy: An Analysis of the Economic Issues*, by Wayne M. Morrison and Marc Labonte.

[49] If Chinese banks raised interest rates in an effort to control inflation, overseas investors might to try to shift funds to China (through illegal means) to take advantage of the higher Chinese rates. The Chinese government has had difficulty blocking such inflows of "hot money." Such inflows force the government to boost the money supply to buy up the foreign currency necessary to maintain the targeted peg. Expanding the money supply contributes to easy credit policies by the banks, which has contributed to overcapacity in a number of sectors, such as steel, and speculative asset bubbles (such as in real estate). This often forces the government to use administrative controls to limit credit to certain sectors.

[50] Private consumption in China has been rising rapidly over the past several years, but not as fast as over parts of the economy.

[51] In comparison, the U.S. figure was 71.1%.

[52] That rate was 43.4% in 1990.

[53] VOX, *The Puzzle of China's Rising Household Saving Rate*, by Marcos Chamon, Kai Liu, and Eswar Prasad, January 18, 2011, available at http://voxeu.org/index.php?q=node/6028.

[54] China Daily, June 6, 2006.

[55] EIA, International Energy Outlook, September 19, 2011, available at http://www.eia.gov /forecasts/ieo.

[56] ExxonMobil, *The Outlook for Energy*, A View to 2030, December 29, 2009, p. 4.

[57] *China's Human Development Report 2005.*

[58] Washington Post, October 29, 2009.

[59] "Highlights of China's Draft 12th Five-Year Plan," *Xinhua*, March 5, 2011.

[60] The MLP identifies main areas and priority topics, including energy, water and mineral resources, the environment, agriculture, manufacturing, communications and transport, information industry and modern service industries, population and health, urbanization and urban development, public security, and national defense. The report also identifies 16 major special projects and 8 "pioneer technologies."

[61] *R&D Magazine*, December 22, 2009.

[62] Sharp increases in Chinese exports of higher-end manufacturing could also raise trade tensions between China and its major trading partners. This has already occurred in some areas, such as wind turbines and solar panels.

[63] For additional information on these issues, see CRS Report R41108, *U.S.-China Relations: Policy Issues*, by Susan V. Lawrence and Thomas Lum.

[64] For a discussion of China's new leaders, see CRS Report R42786, *A Guide to China's Upcoming Leadership Transitions*, by Susan V. Lawrence.

In: China
Editor: Heather A. Collins

ISBN: 978-1-62618-536-4

Chapter 2

THE RELIABILITY OF CHINA'S ECONOMIC DATA: AN ANALYSIS OF NATIONAL OUTPUT*

Iacob N. Koch-Weser

EXECUTIVE SUMMARY

China's recent economic weakness has revived questions about the quality of its economic data. Critics charged that official statistics overstated the economy's growth and understated inflation in China's economy. The recent complaints followed a long period of questioning whether China, a developing country and authoritarian state, has the institutional capacity and political will to publish accurate statistics. Because China is now the world's second-largest economy, and is suffering from economic imbalances, the debate carries more weight than in the past.

This report focuses on China's national output statistics, or gross domestic product (GDP). It concludes that China's official statistics are not as reliable as those produced in the United States and Europe. Several findings support this conclusion. The first is that there are serious deficiencies in the way the Chinese government gathers, measures, and presents its data. Although China's National Bureau of Statistics (NBS)

* This report was released by the U.S.-China Economic and Security Review Commission on January 28, 2013.

now uses sample surveys to measure the economy, survey coverage remains incomplete, particularly in services and the private sector. Economic censuses, in turn, prompt inordinately large revisions of statistical data, and are themselves not on par with international standards. At the same time, many industrial enterprises still report their output directly to the government, keeping in place a Soviet-style reporting system based on state-owned enterprises.

The measurement and presentation of data in China reveals problems as well. Statistical work remains highly decentralized, and the quality and methods of statistical work vary across reporting units in China's vast economy. Other deficiencies are more specific. Measures of consumption rely too heavily on retail sales, while overlooking other forms of consumption. Many of the right laws are now on the books to guarantee accurate reporting of investment, but there is a lack of information to distinguish real investments from those that only exist on paper. Figures on official inflation are even more perplexing. The Chinese government continues to be secretive about the weights it uses to calculate this important measure. The consumer price index, which forms the basis of inflation measures, does not adequately factor in the role of the Chinese service sector and private industry. In addition, China's statistics undergo large and frequent revisions even after they are made public, further calling the government methodology into question.

Manipulation remains an important cause of unreliable statistics. In the past, systemic falsification was more prone to occur during periods of economic and political instability, such as the Asian Financial Crisis in 1998. Nowadays, enhanced scrutiny in- and outside China makes that less likely. Rather, manipulation has become more subtle. In the enterprise sector, both private and state-owned enterprises have incentives to misreport income and output – in some cases to avoid taxes and regulation, in other cases to appease officials. Local officials are not necessarily willing to manipulate statistics simply to overstate economic growth, since they are being evaluated on other performance metrics as well. And yet, anecdotal, statistical, and legal evidence suggests that many local statistics cannot be trusted. The central government would ideally act as a corrective for local-level manipulation, and many experts trust that it is. But Beijing can also tweak data through slight revisions and adjustments. At the very least, the NBS provides too little transparency on how its statistics are calculated.

Further evidence for a lack of reliability lies in the statistics themselves. Alternative measurements of economic activity, such as electricity production and automotive sales, provide a useful way to cross-check official data on national output. An examination of several such alternative indicators over the past decade shows that official statistics mask the volatility, and potentially also the growth rate, of national output since the financial crisis in 2009. Furthermore, there is a marked inconsistency among official statistics. Nominal GDP published at the provincial and national levels does not always add up. Different measures of national output – the production and expenditure methods – are contradictory as well. These incongruities raise the likelihood of inaccurate statistics. To be sure, the Chinese government has made statistical reform a priority over the past thirty years, in the process of transitioning from a Soviet-style command economy to more of a market economy. These reforms are all the more impressive given the rapid structural changes that have taken place in China's economy. China's National Bureau of Statistics has achieved several landmarks over the years, including: the switch to an international system of accounting in 1995; the first national economic census in 2004; and in 2011, the introduction of a seasonally adjusted measure of quarterly GDP growth.

More reliable statistical methods must be put in place to inform officials, the public, and businesses on the risks they face. Such measures could include annual consultations between academic economists and the government. To its credit, the U.S. government has stressed the importance of accurate statistics in dealings with the Chinese government, through both lobbying and technical assistance efforts. For instance, the U.S.-China Joint Commission on Commerce and Trade (JCCT) has repeatedly emphasized the need to harmonize customs statistics on both sides of the Pacific.

Even so, more could be done. The Office of the U.S. Trade Representative, in tandem with its advocacy for China's WTO compliance, could make independent data gathering by foreign and private entities in China a priority. The British bank HSBC has collected independent purchasing managers' indexes (PMI) in China since 2007 – a positive precedent that could be followed elsewhere. The diffusion of best practices is bound to improve the work of China's statisticians at all levels of the reporting hierarchy. The availability of alternative data sources would also reduce the leeway for manipulation. Ultimately, accurate statistics can contribute to the overarching goal of fostering more open, transparent, and market-oriented institutions in China.

INTRODUCTION

Since the 1980s, China has consistently registered high and stable rates of economic growth. Few doubt that China's economy has indeed performed strongly, based on favorable demographics, market reforms, and other factors. And yet, economists have questioned just how accurate economic statistics are in an authoritarian, post-Soviet state undergoing rapid economic restructuring. Is the Chinese government willing and capable of providing accurate statistics? Because China is now the world's second-largest economy, and is suffering from economic imbalances, the answer to these questions is more crucial than ever. Reliable statistics are the foundation for economic analysis, which informs the actions of U.S. businesses and policymakers.

The reliability of China's economic data is questioned in many areas, including unemployment, income distribution, debt, and capital flows.[1] This report focuses on national output, or gross domestic product (GDP). The concern is that official figures do not accurately reflect the rate, stability, and composition of GDP growth. The latest wave of criticism regarding China's statistics came in June 2012. That month, Beijing announced 7.6 percent year-on-year growth for the second quarter of the year, a figure that many analysts considered inflated.[1] Similar concerns surfaced in 2009, when China's economy continued to perform strongly during the global financial crisis.

This report employs two methods to test the reliability of China's national output statistics. The first is to analyze China's statistical work, or how well data is gathered, measured, and presented. China's statisticians continue to be burdened by the institutional legacy of Soviet planning, and by the complexity of a large economy in transition. Moreover, in China's one party state, political manipulation at the national and local level merits scrutiny.

A second method is to conduct "consistency checks". An "external" check – popular among financial analysts – compares official GDP to alternative indicators of economic activity, such as energy use, transport, and automobile sales. Another type of check searches "internally" for discrepancies between different official measures of national output, such as GDP reported by different levels of government. The report draws on diverse sources of data. Official Chinese statistics were culled from the ISI Emerging Markets CEIC China Premium Database. Academic articles on Chinese statistics proved useful, though many are based on data from the 1990s. Western financial media and policy analysis, in turn, provided timely insights on current events. Chinese language sources helped to gauge debates within China. China's statistical work has improved markedly since the 1980s. Nonetheless, there is substantial evidence that China's national output figures continue to be less reliable than in the United States and Europe. External and internal

[1] (1) The unemployment rate is regularly cited as the most inaccurate statistic in China, due to different measurements for rural and urban areas, and the inadequate counting of unregistered urban migrants; (2) Income distribution data is skewed, primarily due to underreported income by wealthy households and migrant workers; (3) National debt levels are hard to measure, in part due off-balance sheet budgets in business and government; (4) China's rising outbound direct investment is distorted by activities like "off-shoring" to tax havens and "round-tripping" through Hong Kong.

consistency checks reveal irregularities. In terms of statistical work, data gathering, measurement, and presentation demonstrate deficiencies in design and execution. There is evidence of political manipulation at the local level, and to some degree, also in the central government. Unfortunately, economists have not debated this complex subject in-depth since the early 2000s. As China's statistics become more vital to U.S. businesses and policymakers, more mechanisms should be put in place to systemically assess their reliability. This could help to better inform relevant actors about potential risks and countermeasures.

SECTION I: THE QUALITY OF STATISTICAL WORK

China's government, led by its National Bureau of Statistics (NBS), has implemented a series of reforms since the 1980s to improve statistical work. Because China was once a Soviet-style command economy, the underlying challenge has been to introduce new methods suited to a market economy, while restructuring the old statistical apparatus. This structural reform has taken place against the backdrop of a rapidly transforming economy. To its credit, the government is now able to present frequent, accurate data on large parts of the economy. However, the pace of reform has slowed under the administration of President Hu Jintao over the past decade. It is also questionable how well the existing laws, regulations, and administrative processes are being implemented. A statement made a decade ago by economist Thomas Rawski, a prominent U.S. economist, still rings true: "The result [of China's reforms] is a statistical edifice that increasingly resembles standard practice in market systems. Ironically, gradual implementation of the new measures does not seem to have improved the accuracy of China's industrial statistics."[2] The following sections explore the ongoing challenges of gathering, measuring, and presenting data in China's statistical edifice. These findings are then qualified by a review of China's ongoing statistical reforms.

Data Gathering

Incomplete Survey Coverage

Surveys are the prevailing method of data gathering in advanced economies. As such, they represent the future of China's statistics. And yet, NBS surveys continue to provide inadequate samples of important sectors of

China's economy. Small-scale businesses in manufacturing and retail are hard to capture, while sectors like transport logistics are almost completely unaccounted for. Although the NBS measures 94 sectors of the economy on an annual basis, it does so for just 17 sectors on a quarterly basis.[3]

Surveys also fail to capture "opaque spots" in the economy. One of the most egregious is household income. In the United States, tax returns provide a proximate indication of household income. Indeed, personal income tax accounts for about 40 percent of U.S. government tax revenue. But in China, the personal income tax in 2011 makes up just six percent of revenue. A big reason for this is that even the wealthiest Chinese households are taxed directly on their wages, but not on their non-wage income, such as real estate, stocks, bonuses, and personal gifts.[4] Households must actively report such income – but many understate their income in tax returns, or refuse to participate in sample household surveys. In this way, they can evade taxes and also avoid the political implications of having excessive wealth in a nominally socialist state. Chinese economist Wang Xiaolu has determined that national spending on real estate, luxury goods, and travel in China implies much higher income among the top 10 percent of earners than is given in official income data.[2] In January 2012, the NBS in fact admitted that it does not publish the Gini coefficient – a leading measure of income inequality - because data on high earners is inaccurate.[5] It is also notable that, in an economy with a large state sector, government officials have only recently begun to disclose their own salaries and wealth to the public, and none are under any legal obligation to do so.[6]

Opacity extends to other sectors as well. Many state-owned enterprises remain secretive about their income statements, especially if they are not publicly listed. New types of large corporate entities, such as fund management companies and real estate arms of conglomerates, often go unaccounted for in both the direct reporting and enterprise survey systems. In local governments, "off-balance sheet" budgets can also skew fiscal revenue and expenditure (Table 1).[7] And in a banking system that heavily favors state-

---

[2] According to Wang, the "grey" economy, already very large, grew significantly after the Chinese government introduced its giant stimulus package in late 2008 in response to the global economic crisis. Using innovative research techniques that bypassed official data, Wang estimated that not only were trillions of renminbi failing to appear in official assessments, but about two-thirds of it belonged to the top 10 percent of the population. He concluded that the rich were hiding their wealth, and society was far more unequal than the government was admitting. Wang Xiaolu, "Woguo Shouru Fenpei Xianzhuang, Qushi ji Gaige Sikao [The Current Status, Trends, and Reform Initiatives Regarding Income Distribution in China]," *Zhongguo Shichang* 20 (2010): 8-19.

owned enterprises, many individuals and small businesses have turned to underground banking networks to access credit.

Table 1. Opaque Areas of the Economy

Unit	Areas Lacking Transparency
Households	Unreported income
Firms	Conglomerate structures and real estate arms
Governments	Off-balance sheet budgets
Banks	Informal credit market

The Outdated System of Direct Reporting

Enterprise revenue determines which firms are eligible for China's direct reporting system. As China's economy grows, so does the number of firms with sizable revenue, which combines to overwhelm the data processing capacity of the NBS. The NBS has tried to reduce the number of firms by continually raising the revenue threshold for direct reporting, among both state-owned enterprises and the non-state sector. When this reform began in 1998, the number of direct reporting firms was decreased from 460,000 to 165,000. However, by 2009, 434,000 firms were again reporting. As of 2011, only firms with annual revenue exceeding RMB 20 million report to the NBS, a measure that has again reduced the number of reporting units (Table 2).[8]

This approach is based on the risky presumption that firms no longer eligible for direct reporting will be adequately accounted for through enterprise surveys. It also "kicks the can down the road" regarding the future of the direct reporting system, which has no place in the statistical work of a modern market economy. Its future sustainability will likely depend on further increasing the reporting threshold. It may also require maintaining a large enough pool of state-owned enterprises, as these are most entrenched in the system.

The Asymmetric Impact of Censuses

To some extent, China's economic censuses have been a success story, since they are incredibly difficult to carry out in a large and developing economy. But they exert a very destabilizing impact on statistics. The 2004 census added a massive 16.8 percent to real GDP. The government argued that this was due to service sector activity that was unaccounted for. A new survey system was subsequently established for 11 service industries, including commerce, real estate, and information technology, and pilot surveys were conducted for small-scale retail, logistics, and gastronomy services. The 2009 national economic census subsequently added 4.4 percent to GDP.[9] Although this was a relative improvement over 2004, it was large enough to raise serious questions about the reliability of annual data. The next economic census, scheduled for 2014, may again lead to major revisions.

Table 2. Direct Reporting Participants

Direct Reporting Participants	Reporting Participants	Number surveyed
Firms Reporting		
1994-1997	All firms village level and above	460,000 (1997)
1998-2006	All SOEs, only private firms with revenue >CNY 5 mn	165,000 (1998)
2007-2010	Only firms with revenue >CNY 5 mn	434,000 (2009)
2011-present	Only firms with revenue >CNY 20 mn	n.a.
Fixed Asset Investments Reported		
1997-2010	Only investments >CNY 500,000	159,000 (1997) 661,000 (2010)
2011-present	Only investments >CNY 5 mn	n.a.

Source: Adapted from Tom Orlik, *Understanding China's Economic Indicators* (Upper Saddle River, NJ: FT Press Science, 2012); Xu Xianchun, "Zhongguo Guomin Jingji Hesuan Tixi de Jianli, Gaige he Fazhan [The Establishment, Reform and Development of China's National Economic Accounting System]" *Zhongguo Shehui Kexue* (China Social Science) 6 (2009): 58-59.

Second, the census does not necessarily provide the most accurate picture of the economy. One issue is the complete enumeration of units – most respondents are surveyed individually by the census takers, and only a few are sampled. The enumeration method is not only costly and inefficient, but also infeasible, given the large number of self-employed persons and labor migrants in the country. Inevitably, many reporting units are overlooked, and that ultimately distorts the results of the census.[10] Another factor affecting census-taking is financing – because a large part of the costs are borne by local governments, and their fiscal capacity varies, the quality of census work is not uniform across China's many jurisdictions.[11]

Data Measurement and Presentation

Consumption and Investment

China's data measurement is deficient in several respects. The first relates to consumption and investment. Over the past decade, China's growth has increasingly shifted toward investment, while household consumption has declined as a share of GDP, and the contribution of net exports has remained roughly constant. The goal of "rebalancing" China's economy therefore hinges on a reduction in investment and increase in consumption. The central question is how dependable the data on these two crucial indicators really is.

China continues to rely on value added by industry as the primary measure of GDP. This measurement adds up the net output of agriculture, industry, and services, focusing on what the economy supplies rather than what it consumes. Most advanced economies, including the United States, prefer the expenditure measure of GDP, which adds up consumption, gross capital formation, and net exports. Most economists consider the latter measure to be superior, because it represents what comes out of the economy that is actually used by citizens, business, government, and the rest of the world.[12]

The NBS does publish expenditure GDP on an annual basis, but only partially. It does not publish inflation-adjusted real GDP growth based on expenditure accounts, nor does it provide expenditure account GDP on a quarterly basis. Consequently, many economists come up with their own erroneous guesstimates. Some critics also suspect that the expenditure figure is adjusted only after the value-added GDP calculation has been done, so that expenditure GDP is arbitrarily adjusted to match the official value-added figure.[13]

Further, the supply-side bias of the value-added GDP figure, combined with the faulty construction of GDP components, serves to skew the measurement of consumption and investment. The implications of this are explored below.

1. Household Consumption

Household consumption measures rely primarily on retail sales data. Other data sources, based on services and household spending surveys, are not sufficiently factored in. Ironically, this crude measurement can serve both to understate and overstate consumption.

Some argue that the retail sales figure itself is overstated because China's statistics tend to measure output more than demand. Retail sales are thus counted when suppliers ship goods to retailers, rather than when goods are actually sold. In other words, unwanted goods may be "dumped in warehouses" but are still valued equally as sold goods.[14]

In its defense, the NBS maintains that official regulations governing statistical work require retail sales to be counted based on sales by wholesalers and retailers.[15] It is hard to tell who is right, since there is little public inventory turnover data available to determine whether warehoused goods are counted in the retail data or not.[16]

Older survey-based studies, done in the 1990s, suggest that actual spending by households does not grow as quickly as official GDP expenditure data.[17]

That finding would corroborate the claim that retail sales exaggerate household consumption. Unfortunately, more recent studies were not found in the process of compiling this report.

Viewed in relation to wages and household savings, retail sales do appear overstated. When consumption rises, as it has in China for most of the past decade, this should be accompanied by a proportionate increase in wages or a decrease in household savings. But as economist Derek Scissors of the Heritage Foundation has noted, retail sales in China continue to outpace personal income, while personal savings have not decreased proportionately.[3] A plausible explanation is that consumption data, based on exaggerated retail sales figures, is inaccurate.

On the other hand, the focus on retail sales may lead to an understatement of consumption as well, because it excludes some of the fastest-growing types of services that are consumed outside the retail sector.[18]

That is a point that the NBS actually likes to emphasize, since it implies that China's economy is rebalancing faster than official figures would indicate. Indeed, NBS researchers recently surveyed housing rents in China's four largest cities to prove this point.

The study found that rents are not fully accounted for in the official consumption measure, especially when undocumented urban migrants are renting.

The survey concluded that, if expenditure on rents in China were measured accurately, national household consumption in 2010 would have been *8 percent* higher. The revision would also increase household

---

[3] For example, in the first half of 2012, personal income grew 13.9 percent, retail sales 14.4 percent, and personal savings 16.4 percent. Derek Scissors, *How the Party Says China's Economy is Doing*. Heritage Foundation, July 13, 2012, http://blog.heritage.org /2012/07/13/how-the-party-sayschinas-economy-is-doing/; Thomas G. Rawski, "What Is Happening to China's GDP Statistics," *China Economic Review* 12 (2001): 347-50.

consumption in China's four largest cities by up to 11 percent. Needless to say, national GDP would be larger as well (Table 3).[4]

Table 3. Impact of Housing Spending on Consumption Rate: Beijing, Shanghai, Guangzhou, Shenzhen, 2010

	Beijing	Shanghai	Guangzhou	Shenzhen	National
Official household consumption rate (%)	32.9	42.4	33.8	41.5	33.8
Spending on Residential Housing (RMB bn)	298.7	215.2	107.0	169.4	2,690.1
Adjusted household consumption rate (%)	43.5	47.9	38.7	49.4	38.9
Adjusted household consumption as share of GDP	17.8	11.3	9.2	15.3	6.5

Source: Adapted from Xu Xianchun et al, "Jumin Zhufang Zuping Hesuan Ji Dui Xiaofulu de Yingxiang (On Residents House Rents and Its Impact on the Consumption Rate)", Kaida *Daobao* (China Opening Journal) 2 (April 2012): 12-15.

2. Fixed Asset Investment

The questions surrounding fixed asset investment are similar to those of household consumption. One allegation is that, due to the supply-side bias of China's GDP measures, investment may be counted when funds are disbursed, rather than when an investment actually results in the use of working capital. If disbursal of funds is recorded as GDP growth, can the government not easily

[4] Spending on housing in China is commonly measured in two ways: (1) Through surveys of residents to assess daily spending habits and the relative weight of basic needs; (2) Through housing spending as share of final consumption in GDP. These methods discount the actual market cost of housing, and provide only a very narrow definition of housing spending. The result is an underestimate of household spending. Xu Xianchun et al, "Jumin Zhufang Zuping Hesuan Ji Dui Xiaofulu de Yingxiang [On Residents House Rents and Its Impact on the Consumption Rate]," *Kaida Daobao* [China Opening Journal] 2 (April 2012): 12-15.

control the pace of growth by the pace at which it releases funds?[19] In its defense, the NBS has pointed to regulations decreeing that investments only be tabulated when working capital is employed.[20] Enforcement of the regulations is hard to verify, because little public data is made available on how investments are utilized.

Infrastructure projects, a core component of fixed asset investment, provide a poignant example of how investment statistics can become unreliable. According to Chinese law, developers are required to build on land they buy within two years. They may therefore tell the government that a project is "under construction," and make only minor investments, so as to avoid having the land confiscated.[21] Rising land sales in recent years are therefore likely to have caused a gross overstatement of investment.[22] Many analysts are forced to look at pre-sales of properties to get any accurate estimate of what properties are actually coming on the market. Only three-quarters of properties in China are pre-sold, though, so that this corrective mechanism is far from perfect.[23]

Prices and Inflation

Inflation is a vital component of national output measurement, because it determines the difference between nominal and real GDP. Yet even here, there are several reasons to question reliability. First, the NBS does not detail how it calculates inflation. China uses a combination of deflators to translate nominal GDP to real GDP. Several indices (or combinations thereof) can be used to arrive at the deflator (e.g. the consumer price index, producer price index, retail price index, etc.). But the NBS does not publish how it arrives at the deflator each year. By contrast, other countries are very transparent about how they compile this data, since it is such a vital signal for investors to gauge inflation. The NBS does not even publish a deflator for its GDP reports.[24] World Bank senior economist Louis Kuijs has also criticized the government's refusal to release details on how much weighing it gives to different product categories when calculating inflation.[25] One of the reasons this matters is that there is an unusually large gap between China's food inflation and general inflation; in other words, low official inflation can mask the price hikes felt by consumers (Figure 1).

A second issue pertains to price indices. Inflation is calculated based on price indices, such as the consumer price index (CPI). To attain CPI, the NBS monitors the prices of products at markets across the country. It puts an unusually large number of products in its CPI basket — according to one account, 262 products compared to 211 in the United States.[26] And yet, the price index is not comprehensive enough; many services, such as IT, accounting, and advertising, are not included in the index.

One indication that China's consumer price indices are dubious is the fact they do not always correlate well with the implicit GDP deflator, which is based on the producer price index. In the first half of 2012, the GDP deflator was 3.2 percent, versus CPI of 3.3 percent. While this matched nicely, in 2010, the GDP deflator was twice as high as the CPI.[27]

A final issue is that state subsidies distort market prices. In the service sector, such distortions have the effect of understating GDP. Welfare services directly provided by SOEs and collectively owned enterprises to employees and their families, as well as subsidized housing, lead to an *underestimation* of value added in services, which is often derived from the income generated by the housing or welfare provider. In turn, in the industrial sector, producer subsidies can lower the market prices of certain goods, and that reduces their official value-added.[28]

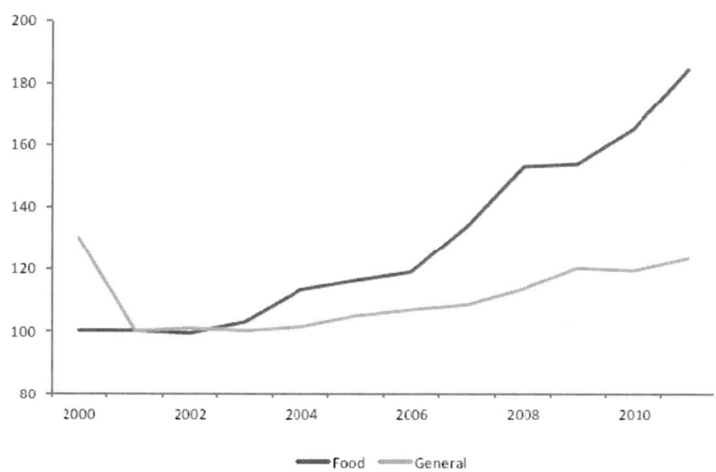

Source: FAOStat.

Figure 1. China's Average Consumer and Food price indices (2000 = 100).

Inflation measures also tend to privilege state-regulated over market-oriented prices. For instance, CPI for services is based primarily on the prices of state-provided health, transport and education, while neglecting the more volatile price trends in private services. Prices may therefore appear more stable than they really are. Data collected by the National Development and Reform Commission (NDRC) – China's premier industrial planning agency –

shows that inflation for medical care and education has been running at 5-10 percent in 2001 to 2012, well above the 1-2 percent figure reported in the NBS's CPI.[29]

Due to the legacy of a planned economy, industrial enterprises may also misreport prices. Long-term real GDP growth should be measured at constant prices, so that the statistics reveal real value created, not just changes in prices. But China's enterprises still suffer from the so-called "comparable price" approach used in the Soviet era. Under this approach, enterprises report their output based on constant prices derived from a "price manual" published every few years. The problem is that in a market economy, new products are constantly introduced into the market. When this happens in years when the price manual is not published, there may not be any reference products in the price manual. This creates leeway for enterprises to exaggerate their real output by categorizing more products as new products and then specifying their current market prices to be close to their "constant prices". If the elapsed time since the creation of constant prices includes periods of inflation, the "constant prices" assigned to the new products can become unrealistically high.[30]

Such reporting deficiencies may be exacerbated by local governments. In the 1990s, studies showed that some provincial and local statistical agencies compiled enterprise output figures based on current prices, deflated the aggregated figures, and submitted the deflated totals to higher-level statistical offices. Although national-level officials suspected that the deflators applied by provinces understated inflation, they did not always adjust them adequately.[31] To some extent, this behavior may persist today.

Measurement across Units

Another major concern regarding China's data measurement is the lack of standardization across units. First of all, in different industries, statistics methods were established at discrete points in time, such that they are now inconsistently measured.[32] To calculate the value-added of industry, government statisticians mix production and income approaches (Table 4).[33] There can also be data mismatches within sectors. In the transport sector, cargo data is more accurate than the financial data of transport companies. In the financial industry, data at traditional banks is more complete than at new types of financial service providers. At the macro-level, statistics are still compiled differently for the urban and rural sectors, even for basic items like household income.[34]

Table 4. Value-added Measures of GDP – Data Availability by Sector

Data quality	Calculation method	Number of sectors	Share of GDP
Annual (94 sectors surveyed)			
Full data available; extrapolation low	Direct calculation of output and value added	51	60%
Partial data; extrapolation medium	Subset calculated and used to impute the rest, using proportion of value added for that sector in last census year (census every five years)	32	35%
Minimal data; extrapolation high	Output and value added estimated based on value in last census year and growth rate of a reference indicator	11	5%
Quarterly (17 sectors surveyed)			
Minimal data; extrapolation high	Estimate based on indicators that should move in line with value added growth during same period in prior year	14	
Minimal data; extrapolation high	Estimate based on output growth and its ratio to value added during same period in prior year	3	

Source: Adapted from Tom Orlik, *Understanding China's Economic Indicators* (Upper Saddle River, NJ: FT Press Science, 2012).

In a 2004 analysis, economist Carsten Holz suggested varying degrees of reliability in each sector of the economy (Table 5).

The NBS's reliance on provincial-level data to obtain nationwide aggregate data introduces further inaccuracies. Local level data may not only be falsified and of low measurement quality; different provinces also tend to differ in terms of the speed at which they adopt new concepts.[35] Local governments may undertake their own reforms; one case is Sichuan province, where the provincial authorities introduced a digital platform in 2007 to unify statistical reporting of companies across sectors. It is unclear how and whether Sichuan's experiment is being implemented elsewhere.[36]

China's survey system is also highly fragmented. The NBS, local government agencies, and State Council ministries conduct their own surveys, which may or may not be coordinated.[37] Companies with operations in several provinces are frequently double-counted, leading to exaggeration of output.[38] The Statistics Law, revised in 2009, was partly designed to avoid overlap of national and provincial survey teams.[39] It remains to be seen how effective the new law will be. Strangely, centralization can be as counterproductive for China's statistical work as decentralization. Although statistical work is fragmented within the government, the government itself, through NBS, has centralized control over the nation's statistics. There is very little parallel collection of statistics by independent agencies. In many advanced economies, non-government actors serve as crucial checks and balances.[40]

Table 5. Reliability of GDP data by sector

	Highly reliable	Somewhat reliable	Unreliable
Primary sector	-	-	100.0%
Secondary sector			
Industry	66.5%	-	33.5%
Construction	56.7%	43.3%	-
Tertiary sector	-	-	-
Transport	60.0%	-	40.0%
Wholesale/retail trade	48.6%	-	51.4%
Banking and insurance	80.0%	20.0%	-
Real estate	-	-	100.0%
Government	-	100.0%	-
All other services	-	50.0%	50.0%

Source: Adapted from Carsten A. Holz, "China's Statistical System in Transition: Challenges, Data Problems, and Institutional Innovations," Review of Income and Wealth 50:3 (September 2004): 404.

The Timing and Revision of Data

A final problem regarding China's statistical data is its hurried release to the public. One oddity is that China is always one of the first countries to report GDP figures, usually only two weeks after the end of each quarter. Most developed economies, which collect smaller volumes of data more efficiently, take between four and six weeks.[41] China's seemingly premature publication of GDP data is a key reason to question reliability. On the other end of the spectrum, an IMF report has noted that many specific datasets, such as balance of payments, are released infrequently or with significant time lags.[42]

In addition to timing, there is a lack of clarity regarding the revisions of published GDP figures. In order for data to be timely, economists frequently publish it in the absence of full information, and later revise it. But in China's case, revisions are frequent, large, and not always clearly explained. One gap that regularly appears is between annual and year-to-date figures. Beijing reports figures at the end of each month, but at year's end, the annual total contains an implicit and substantial revision of the monthly figures. Examples of this are urban fixed asset investment, which tends to be revised downward at year's end, and outbound investment, which tends to be revised upward.[43]

A more serious matter, referenced in the discussion of the census above, is the revision of long-run GDP growth. It originated in 1997, when the NBS partnered with Japan's Hitotsubashi University to revise China's historical growth estimates for the period 1952- 1997, based on the SNA calculation methods. At the time, several academic economists presented evidence that the Hitotsubashi study overstated growth over those decades because it miscalculated price levels and productivity growth. Contrary to the Hitotsubashi study, economist Angus Maddison got an average annual real GDP growth of 2.39 percent for 1978-1995, well below the official rate of 7.49 percent.[44] The controversy that began in 1997 grew more serious in the early 2000s, after a law in 2003 allowed the NBS to undertake revisions of long-run GDP data based on census findings.[45] Two years later, the first national economic census added 16.8 percent to total GDP. The NBS then used this new figure to revise growth at current prices and real GDP for 1993-2004, with the revised annual growth averaging 1.5 percent higher than the original.[46] A common criticism was that the inflation rate and the base years used for the revision were inaccurate. Since official updating was done only with current price information, it is not clear how the NBS adjusted price deflators for this period. In the end, the outcome in real terms involved an increase in annual average real GDP growth from 9.4 to 9.9 per cent for 1992-2003; by contrast, economists Angus Maddison and Harry Wu recalculated a growth rate of just 8.7 percent.[47]

Overview of Statistics Reforms

Challenges of Statistical Work in the Reform Era

China's statistical work faces a dual challenge: a difficult institutional legacy and a complex transition economy. Before 1949, China did not have a unified system of national accounts. After assuming power, the Chinese

Communist Party (CCP) introduced the Soviet Material Product System (MPS) in 1952, adopting statistical methods prevalent throughout the Soviet Union. Political movements like the Great Leap Forward (1958-1961) dealt setbacks to statistical work. Nonetheless, leading experts agree that China's statistics were useful enough for the purposes of a planned economy.[5]

But once China embarked on reform in 1978, the Soviet MPS left several negative legacies for statistical work under a market economy:

- Statistics were designed to measure physical inputs and outputs in a command economy. Demand-side indicators for investment and consumption were not properly measured.[48]
- The economy outside the formal state sector was either discounted or inaccurately measured. In particular, the MPS created a category of "non-material services" that conflated several types of services, including retail sales, real estate, transport, and welfare benefits. It also failed to account for transactions among rural households, and for defense industry production.[49]
- Data gathering was highly decentralized. The central government relied on local statistical bureaus to relay data up the administrative hierarchy. At the central level, different ministries collected and published their own data. Data gathering also relied on "direct reporting" of output by every state-owned enterprise and rural collective; surveys and censuses, the more sophisticated forms of data gathering, were hardly used.[50] More generally, output was measured very differently in the backward rural sector and industry-heavy urban sector.
- In an autarkic, authoritarian state, officials were more preoccupied with pleasing their superiors than informing the general public.[51]

To compound the Soviet legacy, China's statisticians in the reform era confronted an economy in flux:

[5] The standard narrative is that China's statistical performance rapidly improved in 1949-57 but was devastated by the Great Leap Forward, because it was politicized and "plans became dreams." After the Great Leap, however, China's statistics work steadily improved. People's communes and their subdivisions were under continual pressure to produce reliable statistics. There was also a steady increase in rural statistics personnel, helped by expanding literacy and training of accountants. Thomas G. Rawski, "On the Reliability of Chinese Economic Data," *Journal of Development Studies* 12:4 (1976): 438-441.

- Data gathering capacity was weakened by the proliferation of non-state firms, small businesses, and urban labor migrants, as well as by the restructuring of the state sector. While the increase in new enterprises overwhelmed the direct reporting system, the increasing economic activity outside the formal sector was not sufficiently monitored.[6]
- The new market economy required more diverse and sophisticated indicators to track supply and demand. As manufacturing in China became less vertically integrated and more firms procured their components from others, it also became more difficult to discern the value added at each stage of production. That increased the likelihood of upward bias, as the same product was liable to be counted multiple times.[52]
- The added emphasis on economic growth reduced the incentive for firms to devote resources to statistical reporting. In parallel, it provided distorted incentives for officials and managers to manipulate statistics for personal gain.[53]

History of Key Reforms

The Chinese government has implemented a series of reforms since the 1980s (Table 6). In terms of data gathering, the NBS moved from an "all-comprehensive reporting system marred with guesstimates for an increasing share of industry to a two-class data compilation system [...]."[54] On the one hand, it reformed the direct reporting system by introducing a minimum threshold in 1998 to ensure that only firms with large annual revenue would participate.[55] For the rest of the economy, the NBS increasingly relied on surveys and censuses. Prior to the 1990s, China made limited experiments with these methods, but in the 1996 revision of China's Statistics Law, surveys and censuses were codified for the first time as the primary method of data gathering in China. Teams were installed across the country to conduct several types of surveys:

- Weekly price data collection at local markets;
- Annual household surveys in urban and rural areas; and

[6] The share of directly reporting industrial enterprises drops from 100 percent to 5.65 percent in 1986 and 2.07 percent in 1998, and also fell in terms of industrial output value share (90 percent 1979 to 60 percent 1999).

- Surveys of non-state industrial enterprises too small to qualify for direct reporting.[56]

Further, economic censuses complemented surveys by gathering comprehensive data at larger intervals. Beginning in 1985, China conducted national censuses of industry (1985, 1995), services (1993), and agriculture (1996). In 2004 and 2009, the NBS ran its first national economic censuses of industry and services, covering 19 national economic sectors, including the previously opaque construction sector.[57] According to law, national economic censuses are to be undertaken twice a decade, and the next censuses are scheduled for 2014 and 2019.[7] The government also began to do a better job of measuring and presenting the data it gathered. In 1995, Beijing fully adopted the international System of National Accounting (SNA), which is designed to measure indicators of relevance to a market economy.[58] Two years later, the NBS placed statistics on more solid legal footing by codifying methods to calculate and present GDP to the public.[59] It also developed better techniques to impute statistics based on limited sample data. The most recent reform in this regard was a seasonally adjusted measure of quarterly GDP growth, introduced in 2011.[60] In parallel, the government became more open. The publication of the first statistics yearbook in 1982 signaled the beginning of a relaxation of secrecy, and was followed by a "deluge of yearbooks, census materials, surveys, and [...] internet publications".[61] Input-output tables were first published for the whole economy in 1987, and now appear every five years, allowing scholars to better devise their own alternative estimates of GDP growth.[8]

---

[7] The purpose of undertaking economic censuses is to collect information on the secondary and tertiary industries in terms of their development scale, structure and economic performance; establish and maintain the business register and database systems; and lay a solid foundation for research and formulation of the national economic and social development planning and for improving decision-making and management. It plays an important role in reforming the statistical system; improving the national economic accounting system and statistical monitoring, warning and forecasting systems. United Nations Statistics Division. "Economic Census: Challenges and Good Practices: A Technical Report." (October 2010): 14.

[8] Input-output tables (IO tables) are the key way for economists to determine the value-added at different stages of the production process (e.g. from the production of rubber to the sale of a car tire). In advanced economies, IO tables are used in tandem with supply and use tables, which provide a detailed analysis of the structure of the costs of production and income generated in the production process, the flow of goods and services produced within the national economy, and the flows of goods and services with the rest of the world.

Moreover, the government worked with Japan's Hitotsubashi University in 1997 to revise GDP estimates for the period 1952-95, based on the SNA method.[62]

Table 6. Timeline of Statistical Reform in China

Year	Event
1983	National Statistics Law introduced to reduce manipulation of statistics
1984	Consumer price offices introduced at provincial and municipal level to sample data for price indexes
1985	National Bureau of Statistics begins to compile tertiary sector and aggregate production GDP stats
1990	First volume published with national and provincial GDP going back to 1978
1991	First tertiary sector census (lasts from 1991 to 1995)
1993	Official switch to UN System of National Accounts
1995	First secondary (industrial) sector census reveals problems of rural industrial data for first time. Results in a downward revision of up to 25 percent for the gross output value of collective-owned and private enterprises in 1991-1994, and as well as major revisions in production accounts
	Begins reporting according to the UN System of National Accounts (SNA) and discontinues the Soviet Net Material Product (NMP) system
1996	1st Revision of 1983 National Statistics Law drastically reduces the role of the traditional industrial enterprise reporting system in favor of censuses and sample surveys
1997	NBS publishes national accounts for every province for the time period 1952-1995, with expenditure accounts in nominal and real growth terms
	Local government data manipulation comes to a head: (1) February 1998: State Council threatens disciplinary measures if local officials falsify statistics; (2) March 1998: NBS dispatches investigative teams to provinces
	Two laws are issued to codify the calculation of annual and seasonal GDP
1998	Reform of ownership classification results in a new category for state-owned enterprises (SOEs), which provides a very broad definition for the state-owned sector
	Direct reporting system reformed for first time in order to include only larger industrial enterprises

Table 6. (Continued)

Year	Event
1999	NBS increases monitoring of provincial-level statistical work, especially in order to monitor major
2004	First national economic census - GDP revised by 16 percent
2007	Direct reporting system again adjusted to include less firms
2009	Second national economic census - GDP revised by 4 percent
	2nd Revision of National Statistics Law increases punishments for manipulation of statistics
2011	Seasonally adjusted quarter-by-quarter growth metric introduced for the first time (as of 1Q11)
	Direct reporting system adjusted again to include less firms

Source: Various. Adapted from Carsten A. Holz, "China's Statistical System in Transition: Challenges, Data Problems, and Institutional Innovations," Review of Income and Wealth 50:3 (September 2004): 387-95; Tom Orlik, Understanding China's Economic Indicators, 1-62.

Section II: Political Interference

The possibility of political manipulation has been raised not only by outside observers, but also by the Chinese government itself. The key question, however, is how *systemic* and *persistent* it is across units and over time. The sections below aim to provide an analytical framework for discussing manipulation.

Instances of Coordinated Falsification

One theory suggests that China's data becomes less dependable when the economy is in poor shape and officials are afraid to report negative performance. Such instances of mass manipulation are popularly referred to in China as "winds of falsification (*jiabao fukua feng*)". Historical instances of such manipulation are:

- In the Great Leap Forward (1959-62), China suffered extreme declines in agricultural output. Local officials nevertheless overstated production, thus contributing to the worst famine epidemic in the nation's history.[9]

- In the late 1980s, China suffered from high levels of inflation and urban unemployment in the lead-up to the Tiananmen Square massacre in June 1989. Some scholars argue that the economy actually contracted in 1989, counter to official growth figures of over 10 percent.[63]
- During the Asian Financial Crisis in 1998, China recorded 7.8 percent annual GDP growth, down just 1 percent from 1997. This was not only anomalous in the regional context, but also contradicted the sharper decline in more specific economic activity, such as energy consumption and airline travel.[64] Notably, when the NBS revised historical GDP growth rates in 2005, the real GDP growth figure for 1998 was spared any revision.[65]

Since 2009, the global financial crisis and subsequent recession in the global economy may have provided new incentives to manipulate statistics. Under such circumstances, local officials may be even more eager to meet the central government's growth targets, even if their local economies are not performing well.

The incentive to manipulate data in 2012 was arguably magnified by the leadership transition – many officials were due for promotion and so were keen to present a strong economic track record. Predictably, numerous economists questioned China's high growth rates throughout 2009, at the height of the crisis, harkening back to similar criticism during the Asian Financial Crisis in 1998.[66]

Further, in July 2012, China's National Bureau of Statistics (NBS) announced 7.6 percent year-on-year growth in China's GDP for the second quarter of the year.

Although the figure confirmed a sixth straight quarter of declining growth, it was down just 0.5 percent from the previous quarter. Based on weak industrial output, some analysts suggested growth 0.3 percent lower than the official figure.[67]

[9] One study suggests that cadres and officials from different levels, under pressure from upper-level leaders and competing counterparts, over-reported grain output for fear of punishment, contributing to the serious grain shortage and death of millions of people. Yongshun CAI. "Between State and Peasant: Local Cadres and Statistical Reporting in Rural China." *The China Quarterly* 163 (September 2000): 783-805.

Manipulation Along the Reporting Hierarchy

Local Governments

It is useful to be aware of historical moments when China's statistics are more susceptible to coordinated manipulation. The downside of this approach, however, is that it does little to uncover the underlying mechanisms that cause manipulation on a regular basis. To understand these, it is useful to break down manipulation among different units in the chain of statistical work.

It is commonly argued that manipulation occurs most frequently at the local level. Several pieces of evidence back this claim. Over the past decade, the economic growth figures reported by local governments have regularly exceeded those of the central government. There is also anecdotal evidence of malfeasance by individual officials; notably, a deputy governor of Anhui Province tried on corruption charges in 2005 revealed that he had ordered a local planning commission to deliberately overstate GDP growth.[68] In addition, recent policy actions by the central government imply that manipulation does occur. In the 2009 revision of the 1983 Statistics Law, the NBS introduced new punishments for manipulation. During the unveiling of the law, officials spoke extensively about local government malfeasance.[69]

In institutional terms, a particular set of incentives and constraints also encourages statistical manipulation at the local level. In the primary and tertiary sectors, the NBS is heavily reliant on local statistical bureaus. Officials at different levels thus have ample opportunity to manipulate data.[70] Second, there is a lack of checks and balances. The 1983 Statistics Law, promulgated by the NBS, stipulates that local statistical agencies are subject to local governments in administrative affairs. As a result, local governments today still provide the financial support for the statistical agencies, which gives them significant power over personnel appointments. This intertwined relationship may compromise the independence of the agency.[71]

Historically, the enforcement of the Statistics Law has been lackluster. In 1994 and 1997, a series of nation-wide inspections uncovered more than 60,000 violations of the Statistics Law. In spite of the huge number of violations, very few officials were punished by their superiors.[72] The recent 2009 revision, referred to above, sets out harsher and more detailed punishments. During investigations into manipulation, officials can be subjected to a documented interrogation and even face prosecution.[73] But given the poor historical precedents of enforcement, institutional path dependence suggests that local officials will not take enforcement of these laws very seriously.

On the incentive side, economic data may be manipulated to please officials at higher levels of government. In the absence of a democratic electorate, the tenure and promotion of officials is contingent upon superiors.[74] The imperative to satisfy higher-level officials through economic performance likely took hold in the 1990s. In the 1980s, there was still debate about the merits of capitalism, so local governments were reluctant to overstate economic achievements. Chinese officials also had painful memories of the Great Leap Forward disaster, and so took special care to report data accurately.[10] After the Tiananmen Incident, however, increased economic growth became more important to evaluating an official's performance than ideological correctness or honest reporting.[75] Especially in localities with lackluster economic conditions, officials could disguise poor economic performance by manipulating statistics.[76] A popular Chinese idiom, "officials falsify economic statistics because economic statistics determine their achievement (*guanchu shuzi, shuzi chuguan*), even suggests that this is a custom dating back to pre-modern China's mandarin bureaucracy.[77]

Meeting the growth targets set out by the government can play an important role in an official's promotion. One set of targets is officially enshrined in the Five-Year Plans formulated by the central government. According to Rawski, another type of target is implicit – Chinese officials view attainment of "magic 8 percent" GDP growth as a "great political responsibility".[78]

Although local governments constitute the primary source of manipulation, some factors mitigate this problem. For one, provinces with poorer governance and less stable economic conditions are probably more liable to manipulate data. Since such provinces tend to be poorer, they may also be of less import to the national economy. In the provinces where the data matters most, like Shanghai and Guangdong, the likelihood of honest reporting, at least in principle, is greater.

Further, new performance metrics may begin to militate against the need to achieve economic growth at all costs. For example, it is not necessarily in the best interest of local officials to overstate growth, because energy use per unit of GDP is now an important metric to gauge the environmental record of

[10] In 1962, following the Great Leap Forward, the government issued a circular on strengthening statistical work, which led to marked improvements. The Cultural Revolution was politically disruptive, but did witness some modernization of statistics. Dwight H. Perkins, Market Control and Planning in Communist China, Cambridge, MA: Harvard University Press, 1966. Quoted in Carsten A. Holz, "China's Statistical System in Transition: Challenges, Data Problems, and Institutional Innovations," Review of Income and Wealth 50:3 (September 2004): 382.

officials. Overstated growth can actually cause the central government to discourage spending in order to reduce energy use.[79]

A new wave of studies by political scientists also suggests that Chinese officials may be promoted based on metrics other than economic growth. Victor Shih et al. (2012), using a new biographical database of Central Committee members, a previously overlooked feature of Chinese Communist Party (CCP) reporting, and a novel method that can estimate individual-level correlates of partially observed ranks, find no evidence that strong growth performance was rewarded with higher party ranks at any of the CCP congresses since the 1980s. Rather, factional ties with various top leaders, educational qualifications, and provincial revenue collection were more relevant. Similarly, Guang Gao (2009) has argued that strategic fiscal spending by local governments in visible and quantifiable large-scale development projects is more important than economic growth per se.[80] In addition to macroeconomic data, the government's fiscal records merit close analysis as well.

Local Reporting Units

Another source of manipulation stems from firms that misreport their data to the government. Some economists suggest that such manipulation is worse in the non-state sector. Non-state enterprises lack the traditional accounting systems of SOEs, leaving unskilled statisticians to report company statistics.[81] Further, while the state sector is under relatively tight official supervision, no comparable controls exist for the non-state sector.[82] Some firms actually fear that their income data will be divulged to others as a commercial secret. The NBS has recently taken steps to ensure that names of survey respondents are not revealed to the public after statistics are gathered.[83]

Among small non-state enterprises, there is a distorted incentive to underreport income in order to evade taxes.[84] In some cases, such evasion may be a rational calculation when the fines levied for false reporting are set at absolute rather than relative rates. In such cases, the fine may be far less than what would be paid in additional taxes.[85] It is worth noting that private businesses in China often bear the brunt of China's fiscal policies. Until recently, foreign-invested entities paid a lower statutory corporate income tax than domestic companies, while state-owned enterprises were compensated in the form of subsidies and easier access to credit. In addition, enterprises paid a business tax to the local government and a value-added tax to the central government, essentially an overlapping tax structure. In 2012, the government began to pilot a tax reform in Guangdong province to ease the tax burden; time will tell whether this reform will lower the tax burden on private enterprises nationwide, and so mitigate the incentive for manipulation.[86]

Others suggest that, on the contrary, SOEs are more likely to cheat. Since the 1990s, SOEs have begun to devote fewer resources to accurate statistical work, since SOE managers are primarily judged based on sales and profitability.[87] Local governments may also exert indirect pressure on SOEs, such as utility companies, to report false figures that suit official goals. One top corporate executive with access to electricity grid data told the *New York Times* in 2012 that in Shandong and Jiangsu provinces, centers of heavy industry in east-central China, electricity consumption dropped more than 10 percent over a year earlier, but the reporting units reported flat or only slightly rising electricity consumption.[88] Andy Xie, an analyst at HSBC, agreed: "Many businessmen have told me that their governments ask them to misreport data, including electricity consumption, to hide the depth of the slump." SOE managers are wont to jeopardize their careers by reporting negative performance, since personnel appointments are commonly made by the government agency that acts as the SOE's majority shareholder.[89]

The Central Government

A more sensitive question is how much manipulation takes place at the central level. Beijing has certainly acknowledged that manipulation of economic statistics takes place within the government. In a controversial diplomatic cable released by *Wikileaks* in 2011, China's incoming premier Li Keqiang told U.S. officials that China's GDP numbers were "man-made" and therefore only indicative.[90] During an inspection of the NBS in October 2008, Li publicly stated that "China's foundation for statistics is still very weak".[91] The need for adjustment of the Chinese official estimates was further acknowledged by two NBS officials in 2006: "The sheer size of China, together with the limited resources currently devoted to national accounts and the continuation of MPS-oriented statistical procedures, inevitably means that the official GDP estimates are subject to margins of error that are somewhat bigger than for other developing countries and substantially larger compared with most other OECD countries."[92]

But as with corruption and other hot-button issues, it seems more palatable for Beijing to place the blame on local officials. Former premier Zhu Rongji (1997-2002) once complained of "embellishment and falsification" of local GDP figures.[93] Ma Jiantang, the head of the NBS, admitted in January 2010 that local officials frequently inflate GDP growth - though he maintained that the central government figures were lower and more accurate.[94] In fact, starting in 1998, the NBS began to reject provincial data on GDP growth that it dismissed as "cooked local figures", and began using methods to bypass local and provincial governments.[95]

Some outside observers agree that the central government shares little blame. Princeton economist Chow is among those who argue that, since data is used for government decision-making and is subject to review by all members of the National People's Congress, there is little incentive for the central government to fabricate data. It would hurt the credibility of statisticians within the government, and also lead to confusion among officials using different figures.[96] Indeed, the government could not have managed its economy so well over the past three decades without quality data, and China's economic policy generally reflects the published figures.[97] For these reasons, the common allegation that the government keeps "two sets of books" for administration and publicity does not hold either, since it would require the collusion of thousands of officials.[98]

However, the central government, through the NBS, can manipulate statistics in more subtle ways. First, when it "squeezes the water content" out of inflated local statistics, the NBS does not reveal the size of the revisions to the public. The NBS may also "smooth" over GDP data to disguise volatility. Studies by Goldman Sachs and others suggest that "smoothing" effectively underreports growth in boom years and overstates growth in downturns.[99]

As noted above, the NBS is especially secretive about its inflation measures.[100] Some critics thus argue that the NBS concocts "satisfactory" deflators to suit the government's "rule of thumb" real growth targets. It is hard to find systemic evidence to back this claim. But revisions to past GDP data are indicative. In 1995, the NBS used the results of China's first service-sector census to adjust GDP growth figures for the preceding years. Revisions in levels of GDP — for both expenditure and value-added measures — would require substantial revisions in real growth rates as well. However, no such adjustments were made, implying that as revisions were made in levels, exactly compensating revisions were also made in deflators. In the real world, this coincidence is highly unlikely.[101]

Further, in 2005, when the NBS used the results of the first national economic census to revise GDP growth rates for 1992-2004, it left the real GDP growth figure for 1998 unchanged. That was the year when, according to many economists, China's growth was grossly overstated, because the rest of the region was suffering from the Asian Financial Crisis. The NBS was arguably unwilling to concede to international pressure to revise the 1998 figure downwards, but also did not wish to incite further controversy by raising the figure. It thus ensured that, after adjusting the nominal growth rate upward, the real growth rate would remain unchanged.[102]

A more subtle criticism is that the NBS, when faced with a lack of accurate data, is more likely to report false figures than not to publish at all. Carsten Holz has noted that the NBS repeatedly dropped hints of under-reported national tertiary sector value added prior to the national economic census in 2004, but knowingly reported false GDP data for several years.[103]

In sum, although the evidence for local government manipulation is stronger subtle and at times reinforcing manipulation can occur at the central level. At the very least, there is a lack of transparency.

SECTION III: TESTING RELIABILITY

Alternative Indicators

Using Alternative Indicators to Test Statistical Reliability

Alternative indicators are a common method to judge the reliability of official figures. They span a large range, from energy consumption to transport volumes and producer surveys (Table 7). The common advantage of alternative indicators is that they measure very specific activities in the economy, stem from dependable sources, and/or use numbers that are unrelated to prices and currencies. Electricity production and consumption, for example, is frequently referred to as the "gold standard" for measuring economic activity, because it closely tracks industrial output and is measured in kilowatts. China's five largest electricity generation companies together produce about half of the country's electricity, which makes the data easier to aggregate and harder to manipulate.[104]

Alternative indicators are a popular measuring tool among financial analysts, who are often cited in the media. Among scholars, Rawski set a precedent by using drops in airline travel and electricity consumption to question China's GDP growth figures during the Asian Financial Crisis in 1998.[105] Even senior officials in the Chinese government have acknowledged the usefulness of alternative indicators. In 2007, China's future premier Li Keqiang indicated electricity consumption, rail cargo volumes, and bank lending as his preferred measures of economic activity, in place of official

GDP.[106] The NBS has made tentative efforts to compare China's national output figures with alternative indicators.[11]

A decade ago, several studies were done on alternative indicators, but the results were somewhat inconclusive. In an influential study, Wang Xiaolu and Meng Lian (2001) calculated the physical output of 168 industrial commodities in 1991-1999. They found that output was much lower than official GDP growth would suggest.[107] Yet other scholars found contrary results. Lawrence R. Klein and Suleyman Ozmucur (2003) used a comprehensive set of 15 indicators, ranging from transport volumes to wages,[12] to infer that official GDP growth was indeed reliable for the period 1980-2000.[108] Their findings were supported by Princeton economist Chow, a leading expert on the subject.[109]

While this report cannot match the breadth of these earlier studies, it compares real GDP growth with a number of popular alternative indicators (See Figures 1 to 6 in Appendix). Each figure juxtaposes the year-on-year quarterly growth of an indicator (e.g. from the first quarter of 2008 to the first quarter of 2009) with China's official real GDP.

Table 7. Examples of Alternative Indicators

Category	Alternative Indicator	Unit of measurement	Source
Transport	Air travel	Persons millions	Civil Aviation Administration of China
	Rail cargo	Ton-kilometers millions	Ministry of Railways
	Highway transport volumes	Persons millions	Ministry of Transport
Retail	Auto sales	Units	China Association of Automobile Manufacturers

[11] According to an NBS staff economist, the agency has recently begun to compare GDP, industry value-added, fixed asset investment, retail sales, and disposable household income to other indicators, including fiscal and tax revenue, electricity generation and consumption, inventory turnover, and the scale of savings and loans. Xianchun XU, "Dangqian Woguo Tongji Gaige yu Jianshe de Ruogan Jucuo (Several Measures Regarding China's Statistics Reform and Infrastructure," *Gaige Jianyan* 10 (2011).

[12] The analysis covers energy, transport, communications, labor, agriculture, trade, public sector, wage, and inflation.

Category	Alternative Indicator	Unit of measurement	Source
Survey of business views on current operating conditions and immediate outlook	CFLP Purchasing managers index	Index (>50 expansion, <50 contraction)	China Federation of Logistics and Purchasing (CFLP)
	HSBS/MarkIt Purchasing managers index	Index (>50 expansion, <50 contraction)	HSBC and Markit Economics
	China business survey	Index (>50 expansion, <50 contraction)	Market News International
Energy output and consumption	Electricity output and consumption	KwH millions	National Bureau of Statistics, China Electricity Council
	Coal stockpiles	Tons millions	National Bureau of Statistics, Ministry of Commerce
	Oil and petrochemicals	Tons millions	National Bureau of Statistic
Construction activity	Area under construction	Square meters	National Bureau of Statistics
	Total floor space sold	Square meters	
Intermediate inputs	Brick and concrete pilingproduction	Tons millions	National Bureau of Statistics
	Cement output	Tons millions	National Bureau of Statistics
	Iron ore, steel, and coke consumption	Tons millions	China Iron and Steel Association
Credit policy and activity	Reserve ratio requirement	Percentage	The People's Bank of China
	Benchmark deposit and lending rates	Percentage	The People's Bank of China
	Bank lending in proportion to benchmark interest rate	Percentage	The People's Bank of China
	Bank lending growth	Percentage	The People's Bank of China
	Money supply (M1 / M2)	Renminbi billions	The People's Bank of China

The figures provide some evidence that official real GDP growth for 2012 is unreliable. Several indicators - electricity production, crude oil production, rail turnover, automotive sales, and gross industrial output – witness sharp drops beginning in 2010 that were not reflected in real GDP growth, which remained remarkably stable. It is noteworthy that the degree of decline in many indicators in early 2009, at the height of the financial crisis, was much steeper than real GDP growth would indicate.

To be sure, each indicator's long-term correlation with real GDP growth varies significantly; in the case of automobile sales and output in the iron and steel industry, volatility makes it especially difficult to distinguish any "abnormal" patterns during an economic downturn. Nonetheless, the indicators provide strong grounds to suspect at least an excessive "smoothness" of GDP growth, and perhaps even overstated growth after 2009.

A Note of Caution about Alternative Indicators

Alternative indicators are a useful way to test reliability. But there are also potential disadvantages that analysts must take into account. These include:

- *The quality of data sources varies.* As Table 7 illustrates, the sources for alternative indicators run the gamut from manufacturers associations (e.g. automobiles, iron and steel) to government regulators (e.g. civil aviation), federations, the central bank, and ministries. In some cases, the official source is the National Bureau of Statistics, but the data is based on reports by companies and individuals (e.g. construction activity).
- *As the economy's structure changes, alternative indicators can become less indicative.* For instance, as light industry and services assume a larger share of GDP, the use of heavy industry inputs like coal and steel begins to say less about the overall economy. Electricity consumption in the services and logistics sectors outpaced total power consumption in the first half of 2012. A rising share of residential electricity use could also impact consumption cycles – during a hot summer, homes consume more power, leading to a rise in demand that has little to do with the health of the economy.[110]
- *The performance of alternative indicators is influenced by factors other than economic growth.* Productivity gains can explain drops in consumption. Therefore, decreases in power consumption can be attributed to gains in energy efficiency.[111] Supply and demand dynamics also play a role. Hence, coal stockpile variation is

influenced not just by shipments to power stations (demand) but also by incoming deliveries from suppliers (supply).[112]

- *Different indicators indicate the health of the economy at different points in time.* It is sometimes hard to determine whether an indicator reflects economic trends in the present ("coincident"), or rather in the future ("leading") or past ("lagging"). The common wisdom is that business surveys (e.g. purchasing manager's indexes) are predictive; energy, transport, and industrial activity are coincident; and fiscal and monetary policies are "lagging" (i.e. reacting to the state of the economy). However, in China's case, monetary policies can in fact play a major role in boosting growth, to the extent that they become "leading" indicators. Further, coincident indicators may say more about medium-term than short-term growth. Thus, electricity consumption fell in the first half of 2009, even as the economy grew at an annualized rate of over 7 percent; yet the long-run power consumption growth rate for 2010-2011 was consistent with GDP growth.[113] Moreover, certain indicators are seasonal. Hotel occupancy rates are one example – in 2010-2012, they increased and declined in a predictable yearly cycle. Without seasonal adjustment, such indicators can be misleading.
- *The volatility of growth varies by indicator.* Car sales, for instance, may grow or decline very sharply in the course of a given year. The growth of money supply, on the other hand, is more stable. Comparing either of these to GDP growth has very different implications.

Inconsistencies in China's National Output Data

Another way to assess the reliability of China's economic statistics is to consider them at "face value". Inconsistencies within the data can imply a lack of accuracy, even if it is hard to identify where exactly the source of the error lies. The analysis below looks at discrepancies between different methods of calculating GDP, and between GDP reported at the national and provincial levels.

Production (Value-Added) vs. Expenditure GDP

Different measures of national output – the production measure based on the value-added of industry and the expenditure measure based on consumption and investment (Figure 2) - should add up to roughly the same number, in terms of growth and absolute value. Even in the United States, there is a slight discrepancy between these figures; yet the divergence should be around two percent at most. The difference between the two figures in China, in nominal terms, exceeds the accepted threshold (Table 1 in Appendix). Expenditure GDP is consistently larger in absolute terms, while production-side GDP has shown faster growth in most years. Xu Xianchun, an economist at the NBS, claims that the gap has shrunk, reaching a level on par with the United States in 2007-2009 (Table 2 in Appendix). His figure is based on inflation-adjusted rather than nominal GDP. It remains open to question why the inflation-adjusted figures are so much more congruent than the nominal figures.

Expenditure method. GDP is the sum of final purchases. This is known as demand-side estimation. It finds textbook expression in the accounting definition.

$$GDP = C(consumption) + I(investment) + G(gov't\ purchases) + X(exports) - M(i$$

Income method. GDP is the sum of income payments to the original factors of production:

$$GDP = W(wages) + IN(interest) + P(profits) + R\left(\frac{rent}{royalty}\right) + IT(indirect\ tax) - S(subsidies)$$

Production method. GDP is the sum of value-added across all sectors of production. Value-added is written as:

$$GDP = GP(gross\ production) - IP(intermediate\ production) = VA(value\ added)$$

Figure 2. Methods of Calculating Gross Domestic Product.

Provincial vs. National GDP

National aggregate GDP should be equal to the sum of GDP of each province in China. However, there is a serious discrepancy between nominal GDP at the provincial and national level (Tables 3.1 and 3.2 in Appendix). Provincial GDP figures over the past decade have been significantly higher than those reported at the central level. This fact may corroborate the allegation that local governments like to overstate their economic growth. However, this conclusion is somewhat simplistic. Until 2001, national GDP was actually greater than the sum of provincial GDP. The central government since 2002 may therefore have adjusted provincial GDP figures downwards "automatically", based on the assumption that these figures are always too high. A closer look at Tables 3.1 and 3.2 also shows that the degree of divergence between provincial and national GDP figures varies by sector and type of GDP measurement. When an expenditure measure of GDP is used, the most significant overstatement of provincial GDP is for gross capital formation; in other words, local governments overstate how much investment is taking place in the economy. On the consumption side, the provincial GDP is also overstated, but much less so. In this case, the conundrum is that the gap between provincial and national consumption GDP increased every year in 2005-2010. This strange trend may be led back to the government's efforts to realign provincial and national GDP in 2005, after reviewing the results of the first national economic census (See "Key reforms" section). It appears that this realignment began to fall apart in the ensuing years, as the local government began to overstate consumption more with each year. A production measure of GDP – the preferred measurement used by the Chinese government – reveals other incongruities. In the years leading up to the 2004 national economic census, provincial GDP was hugely overstated in retail and transport. But after 2005, the difference shrank dramatically. One theory, suggested by a journalist at the *Economist,* is that local governments are better able to gauge the true size of the tertiary sector (which includes services like retail and transport). That could be the reason why provincial tertiary sector GDP was so much greater before 2005.[114] After the census, the NBS may have acknowledged that by raising central GDP figures for the tertiary sector to be more in line with the provincial numbers. Since then, retail and transport figures have been more closely aligned. Yet oddly, over that same period since 2005, the gap appears to have migrated to industrial output – provincial figures for industrial sector GDP began to exceed those of the central government. The divergence between provincial and national GDP is a complex problem because it varies across units and over time. It is hard to argue that local governments are always to blame. At least some culpability also belongs to the central government.

SECTION IV: THE DEBATE ON CHINA'S STATISTICS

International Debate

Reliable economic statistics benefits not only businesses and policymakers, but also the public, which has the right to know the truth about the economy. The provision of this public good should be universal. To ensure that it is provided in China, a developing country and one-party state, close scrutiny and informed debate are essential.

As China's economic footprint has grown, the country's official statistics have come under wider scrutiny. The most outspoken authority on the subject is Tom Orlik of the *Wall Street Journal*— his 2011 book, *Understanding China's Economic Indicators*, is the first to explain China's statistics to a broader public.[115] Although the book offers important technical insights, it is more descriptive than analytical, and supports Orlik's claim that "China's economic statistics are actually very impressive, with relatively timely, accurate, and comprehensive data published on a range of key indicators."[116]

By contrast, the *New York Times*, *Foreign Policy*, *Economist*, and other publications have made less favorable assessments. They draw on the skepticism of financial analysts, such as Stephen Green of Standard Chartered Bank, who have distrusted China's official statistics for many years.[117] In policy circles, economists at the International Monetary Fund (IMF) and World Bank have criticized the transparency of work at China's National Bureau of Statistics (NBS). Others, such as John H. Makin (American Enterprise Institute) and Derek Scissors (Heritage Foundation), dismiss the reliability of China's GDP data altogether.[118]

However, the quantity of debate has not been matched by quality. The last time that economists engaged in broad and in-depth analysis was in the late 1990s to early 2000s. At the time, China's statistical work was undergoing radical reform, in line with other promising market reforms ahead of WTO accession. China's long-run GDP growth figures, dating back to the 1950s, were being revised, inciting debates about decades of economic performance. Further, China's economy performed surprisingly well during the Asian Financial Crisis (1997-1998), which led many to charge that the government manipulated GDP figures (see "Political Interference" section). Scholars took a closer look at statistics in diverse industries, from cement production to grain output. Seasoned China economists, such as and Thomas Rawski (University of Pittsburgh) and Gregory Chow (Princeton University), attacked and defended reliability.[13]

Unfortunately, this informed debate has waned in recent years. Prior to the global financial crisis in 2009, China's rapid and stable economic growth

---

[13] The Review of Income and Wealth, a small economics journal, has published much of the relevant scholarship. For an overview, see Carsten A. Holz, "China's Statistical System in Transition: Challenges, Data Problems, and Institutional Innovations," Review of Income and Wealth 50:3 (September 2004): 382.

prompted less scrutiny. With the exception of the 2004 national economic census, the pace of statistical reform was also more incremental. Now, as China confronts serious rebalancing in the years ahead, the quality of statistics is likely to become a point of contention once again.

Civil Society Pressure in China

In theory, civil society is an important force that can pressure governments to be more accountable. In China's authoritarian state, the strength and efficacy of civil society is constrained. Even so, it is important to consider whether any civil society movements are leading to improvements in China's economic statistics.

Economists at semi-autonomous universities and think tanks have criticized the government's statistical work since the 1990's: Huang Yiping (Beijing University) has alleged that the NBS is cognizant of the errors in its own statistics; Wang Xiaolu (National Economic Research Institute), mentioned earlier in this report, has exposed unreported household income among China's richest households; and Yue Ximing (Chinese Academy of Social Sciences Bureau of Economics) has published a litany of academic papers on faulty reporting in the service sector. Wang and others are also engaging with Western critics on these subjects.[14][119] However, partly owing to constraints on free speech, China's scholars prefer to focus on technical rather than political aspects.

To be sure, the Chinese government is debating its statistical work with independent economists. Xu Xianchun, a staff economist at the NBS, has acted as a public ambassador of his institution over the past decade, publishing numerous academic articles in both Chinese and English. Xu has time and again questioned the reliability of China's official figures. However, his underlying claim is that the NBS's measurements *understate* rather than overstate GDP growth. That, of course, is a viewpoint that China's leadership is prepared to accept.[120]

A more interesting phenomenon to observe is how the broader public exerts pressure on the government. Chinese newspapers have long criticized

---

14 Examples of Chinese academics engaging with the West on the subject of economic data: (1) Wang Xiaolu has been interviewed by the *International Herald Tribune* on hidden household income; (2) Huang Yiping has given a speech supporting critical findings in an article in *Foreign Policy* magazine; and (3) Xu Xianchun issued a retort to an American Enterprise Institute report claiming that China's GDP figures are bogus.

the manipulation of data by local officials.[121] This is likely of less concern to the central government, since it has openly acknowledged that this occurs. What really catches Beijing's attention is when the public attacks statistics published at the national level. In February 2009, the NBS's release of its 2008 National Statistics Bulletin caused a public uproar, because it blatantly understated the appreciation in housing prices. In light of China's real estate bubble at the time, the false number was highly controversial. The NBS eventually relented, publishing data to show that average housing prices had actually risen by 24 percent.[122]

In December 2009, a staff writer for *Xinlang Caijing*, a popular online finance publication, cited critiques of China's statistical work listed in an IMF staff report. The revelation prompted strong reactions from Chinese bloggers. The NBS responded with a statement that the IMF did not agree with the blogger's representation of its findings.[123]

These instances illustrate that the public is exerting pressure on the central government, to the extent that the latter feels compelled to justify its methods and weigh in on major disputes.

CONCLUSION

China's national output figures are not as reliable as those of the United States and Europe. Although alternative indicators and internal consistency checks are imperfect methods, they serve to cast doubt on the quality of data. A closer analysis of China's statistical work sheds light on some of the underlying problems facing China's statistics. These problems stem in part from the lack of reform since the 1990s. With the exception of certain breakthroughs, such as seasonally adjusted growth, there has not been any deeper reform. The lack of reform of statistical work appears to follow a broader pattern during the decade-long administration of President Hu Jintao: a wide range of reforms, from corporate ownership to social welfare, were less ambitious than under the preceding government of President Jiang Zemin.

How committed the Chinese government is to improving statistics is unclear. If improved data indicates, say, a higher share of consumption in GDP, or faster GDP growth, that is conducive to the government's message. The NBS itself is pioneering many of these studies. On the other hand, accurate statistics can also shed light on sensitive problems, like vast income gaps. The government's attempts to conceal the poor quality of air in China's largest cities, and the subsequent loss of public confidence in the government's credibility, illustrate the pitfalls of official mendacity.

The reliability of China's statistics is also a crucial challenge for the world economy. China remains a very open economy heavy reliant on both exports and imports. It is also the primary destination of foreign direct investment worldwide. Countless firms, not to mention their shareholders and creditors, depend heavily on accurate statistics to make decisions.

To its credit, the United States has already taken several actions to improve China's statistics.

- In the 1980s, the estimation of China's economic growth rate received guidance from U.S. economist Irving Kravis through the LINK Project, under the auspices of the U.S. National Academy of Sciences, American Council of Learned Societies, and the Social Science Research Council.[124]
- In 2003, the International Monetary Fund's Statistics Department (STA) launched a technical assistance and training program for government statisticians in China. In March 2009, an STA mission visited China to evaluate the progress of the program; elicit China's views on how to broaden and enhance the technical cooperation between STA and China; and to establish training priorities for 2009-2011.[125]
- In 2009-2011, the U.S.-China Joint Commission on Commerce and Trade (JCCT) repeatedly announced the goal of establishing a "work plan [...] to extend the statistics dialogue and research already conducted under auspices of the JCCT". This goal, however, is confined to trade statistics, and moreover, aims "not to change the official statistics reported by either country, but to understand better the data and methodologies used in the collection and compilation of those official trade statistics".[126]
- According to the NBS, the seasonal adjustment growth statistics that Beijing adopted in 2011 were implemented with technical assistance from the U.S. government.[127]

In addition to assisting China to improve its statistics, the U.S. government should take steps to encourage data gathering by foreign and private entities in China, and lobby the Chinese government to enable this through new regulatory frameworks. The British bank HSBC has collected independent purchasing managers' indexes in China since 2007, in many ways complementing similar efforts by the Chinese government. This precedent should be followed elsewhere.

Also, U.S. policymakers and businesses need to be briefed on the risks they face in relying on Chinese statistics. Such briefings could help to cross-check claims made about Chinese statistics in the Western media, in order to shed light on the areas that really matter.

The debate must move beyond a simple dichotomy between "reliable" and "unreliable"– the quality of China's data should be considered across units and over time. Where there is a problem, we need to better identify whether it was owing to technical failure or not. If it is indeed an issue of manipulation, we need to determine where along the hierarchy – at the individual, local, or central level – the manipulation is in fact occurring.

APPENDIX

Table 1. Difference between Production and Expenditure Measurements of GDP – Nominal GDP and GDP growth

	GDP value (RMB bn)			Annual growth rate		
	Expenditure GDP	Production GDP	Percentage Difference	Expenditure GDP	Production GDP	Percentage Difference
1996	7,416	7,118	4.0%			
1997	8,166	7,897	3.3%	10.1%	11.0%	-0.8%
1998	8,653	8,440	2.5%	6.0%	6.9%	-0.9%
1999	9,113	8,968	1.6%	5.3%	6.2%	-0.9%
2000	9,875	9,922	-0.5%	8.4%	10.6%	-2.3%
2001	10,903	10,966	-0.6%	10.4%	10.5%	-0.1%
2002	12,048	12,033	0.1%	10.5%	9.7%	0.8%
2003	13,663	13,582	0.6%	0.8%	12.9%	0.5%
2004	16,080	15,988	0.6%	17.7%	17.7%	0.0%
2005	18,744	18,494	1.3%	16.6%	15.7%	0.9%
2006	22,271	21,631	2.9%	18.8%	17.0%	1.9%
2007	26,656	26,581	0.3%	19.7%	22.9%	-3.2%
2008	31,598	31,405	0.6%	18.5%	18.1%	0.4%
2009	34,877	34,090	2.3%	0.4%	8.5%	1.8%
2010	40,282	40,151	0.3%	15.5%	17.8%	-2.3%

Source: National Bureau of Statistics, via CEIC data.

Table 2. Difference between Production and Expenditure Measurements of Real GDP – National Bureau of Statistics Version

	2001	2002	2003	2004	2005	2006	2007	2008
United States								
Expenditure approach (1)	1.1	1.8	2.5	3.6	3.1	2.7	2.1	0.4
GDP growth rate (%)								
Production approach (2)	0.8	1.6	2.5	3.6	2.9	2.8	2.0	1.1
GDP growth rate (%)								
Difference (1) - (2)	0.3	0.2	0.0	0.0	0.2	-0.1	0.1	-0.7
China								
Expenditure approach (1)	8.3	9.1	10.0	10.1	11.3	12.7	14.2	9.6
GDP growth rate (%)								
Production approach (2)	9.7	10.7	11.9	12.1	13.4	13.7	13.9	9.8
GDP growth rate (%)								
Difference (1) - (2)	-1.4	-1.6	-1.9	-2.0	-2.1	-1.0	0.3	-0.2

Source: Xu Xianchun, "Zhunque Lijie Zhongguo Jingji Tongji (An Accurate Understanding of China's Economic Statistics)," JingjiYanjiu (Journal of Economic Research) 5 (2010): 26.

Table 3.1. Percentage Difference between Provincial and National Figures – Nominal GDP – Expenditure Method

	Total GDP	Gross Capital Formation	Final Consumption Expenditure		
			Total	Government	Household
1996	-8.3%	2.6%	-14.2%	-21.7%	-12.7%
1997	-6.2%	9.7%	-13.0%	-19.5%	-10.9%
1998	-4.4%	16.2%	-13.5%	-17.9%	-12.6%
1999	-3.0%	14.8%	-13.4%	-15.4%	-14.0%
2000	-0.2%	19.0%	-12.7%	-13.6%	-13.9%
2001	-0.4%	15.2%	-11.6%	-7.6%	-13.8%
2002	0.2%	12.0%	-8.2%	-1.7%	-12.1%
2003	2.0%	10.8%	-4.8%	6.1%	-10.3%
2004	4.2%	13.5%	-2.5%	10.7%	-9.1%
2005	6.1%	22.2%	-0.5%	1.0%	-1.0%
2006	4.9%	21.5%	0.0%	2.2%	-0.8%
2007	4.9%	23.9%	0.4%	4.3%	-0.9%
2008	6.4%	23.3%	1.3%	5.8%	-0.2%
2009	5.0%	21.4%	1.5%	6.7%	-0.4%
2010	8.7%	25.8%	3.9%	7.7%	2.4%

Source: National Bureau of Statistics, via CEIC data.

Table 3.2. Percentage Difference between Provincial and National Figures – Nominal GDP – Production Method

	Total GDP	Primary Industry	Secondary Industry			Tertiary Industry				
			Total	Industry	Construction	Total	Retail	Transport	Finance	Real estate
1996	-4.3%	-2.4%	-8.3%	-7.5%	-13.1%	0.4%	--	--	--	--
1997	-2.8%	0.1%	-6.8%	-6.9%	-6.1%	1.4%	--	--	12.0%	-31.5%
1998	-1.7%	-0.1%	-4.0%	-4.6%	0.1%	0.4%	--	--	10.5%	-30.1%
1999	-1.2%	-1.3%	-3.0%	-4.0%	4.0%	0.9%	--	--	9.9%	-25.8%
2000	-0.5%	-0.8%	-2.5%	-3.7%	6.5%	1.7%	25.9%	21.2%	8.8%	-20.5%
2001	-0.8%	-1.8%	-1.9%	-3.5%	9.7%	0.6%	25.8%	25.5%	0.2%	-17.3%
2002	0.4%	-2.1%	0.2%	-1.5%	12.8%	1.3%	27.4%	27.3%	1.6%	-15.3%
2003	2.7%	-1.4%	4.0%	2.3%	16.0%	2.5%	27.0%	33.2%	5.1%	-12.5%
2004	5.0%	-3.1%	8.4%	7.1%	17.9%	3.7%	29.3%	33.9%	7.3%	-10.9%
2005	7.7%	1.3%	11.2%	11.0%	12.8%	5.6%	33.7%	25.6%	--	-0.2%
2006	7.6%	0.4%	11.7%	12.3%	7.2%	4.8%	13.2%	8.9%	2.0%	-2.6%
2007	5.2%	-0.1%	10.4%	11.7%	0.7%	0.8%	4.3%	4.6%	-2.4%	-10.7%
2008	6.1%	-0.6%	12.2%	14.0%	0.1%	0.9%	0.9%	8.7%	-1.7%	-9.0%
2009	7.2%	0.0%	14.1%	16.5%	0.0%	1.4%	10.2%	10.3%	1.3%	-8.4%
2010	8.8%	0.0%	17.4%	20.3%	0.3%	1.6%	10.1%	12.6%	3.0%	-15.0%
2011	10.0%	-0.6%	19.9%	23.3%	-0.1%	1.7%	7.7%	12.4%	--	--

Source: National Bureau of Statistics, via CEIC data.

End Notes

[1] Simon Rabinovitch, "China Figures Prompts Doubts Over Accuracy," *Financial Times*, July 13, 2012.

[2] Thomas G. Rawski. "China by the Numbers: How Reform Affected Chinese Economic Statistics." (Paper presented at conference "Key Issues in China's Economic Development and the Use of Statistical Data", May 2000): 7.

[3] In Shaoxing municipality in Zhejiang province, for example, survey teams must account for 6,000 small and medium-sized enterprises, about one-third in services. Jianmei QI et al., "Jiaqiang Tongji Jichu Gongzuo, Quebao Shuju Zhenshi Kexin [Strengthen Grassroots Statistics Work, Guaranteeing Authenticity and Credibility of Data]," *Zhejiang Tongji* (Zhejiang Journal of Statistics) 8 (2007): 43-44; Orlik, *Understanding China's Economic Indicators*, 5; XU, "The Establishment, Reform and Development of China's National Economic Accounting System," 57.

[4] Deutsche Bank, *China Strategy: Reforms after Leadership Transition* (November 2012): 20-22.

[5] "WSJ Blog/China Real Time: Inside China's Gross Domestic Product Data," *Dow Jones International News*, April 17, 2012; Didi Kirsten Tatlow, "The Hiding that Feeds an Income Gap," *The International Herald Tribune*, January 26, 2012.

[6] Deutsche Bank, *China Strategy*, 26-27.

[7] Xianchun XU, "Zhongguo Guomin Jingji Hesuan Tixi de Jianli, Gaige he Fazhan [The Establishment, Reform and Development of China's National Economic Accounting System]" *Zhongguo Shehui Kexue* (China Social Science) 6 (2009): 58-59; Xianchun XU, "Dangqian Woguo Tongji Gaige yu Jianshe de Ruogan Jucuo (Several Measures Regarding China's Statistics Reform and Infrastructure)," *Gaige Jianyan* (Reform Experiment) 10 (2011).

[8] Tom Orlik, *Understanding China's Economic Indicators: Translating the Data into Investment Opportunities* (Upper Saddle River, N.J.: FT Press, c2012), 24-25.

[9] Orlik, *Understanding China's Economic Indicators*, 16-17; XU, "The Establishment, Reform and Development of China's National Economic Accounting System," 54.

[10] United Nations Statistics Division, *Economic Census: Challenges and Good Practices: A Technical Report* (October 2010): 14.

[11] Ibid, 15.

[12] Albert Keidel, "China's GDP Expenditure Accounts," *China Economic Review* 12 (2001): 355.

[13] Ibid, 355-367.

[14] Jordan Calinoff, "How China Cooks Its Books," *Foreign Policy*, September 3, 2009; John H. Makin, *China: Bogus Boom?* American Enterprise Institute (August 2009), 2. Retrieved from http://www.aei.org/files/2009/08/01/08-EO-Aug-2009g.pdf.

[15] Xianchun XU, "Zhunque Lijie Zhongguo Jingji Tongji (An Accurate Understanding of China's Economic Statistics)," *Jingji Yanjiu* (Journal of Economic Research) 5 (2010): 22-28.

[16] Makin, *China: Bogus Boom?*, 1-4.

[17] Keidel. "China's GDP Expenditure Accounts," 355-367.

[18] "An Aberrant Abacus," *The Economist*, May 1, 2008.

[19] Makin, *China: Bogus Boom?*, 1-3.

[20] XU, "An Accurate Understanding of China's Economic Statistics," 22-28.

[21] Peter Ford, "China Reports Solid Economic Growth: Should We Believe It?" *The Christian Science Monitor*, January 18, 2012.

[22] "An Aberrant Abacus," *The Economist*, May 1, 2008.

[23] Thomas Gatley and Rosealea Yao, "Nearing the Peak," *China Economic Quarterly* 16:4 (December 2012): 12-14.

[24] Donna Caradarelli, "A Closer Look at How China Calculates GDP (Part III)," *EastPoint China Consulting*, February 23, 2012. Retrieved from www.eastpointcc.com/gdp_part3/.

[25] Dexter Roberts, "Foot Massage Doubles and Chinese Doubt Official Price Data," Bloomberg News, August 25, 2010.

[26] "Price Collector Gives Us Food for Thought," *China Daily*, November 9, 2011.

[27] Scissors, *How the Party Says China's Economy is Doing*.

[28] Xianchun XU, "Study on Some Problems in Estimating China's Gross Domestic Product," *Review of Income and Wealth* 48:2 (June 2002): 205-215.

[29] "An Aberrant Abacus," *The Economist*, May 1, 2008.

[30] Gary H. Jefferson, Thomas G. Rawski and Yuxin ZHENG. "Chinese Industrial Productivity: Trends, Measurement Issues, and Recent Developments?" *Journal of Comparative Economics* 23 (1996): 162-163; Angus Maddison and Harry X. Wu. "Measuring China's Economic Performance: How Fast Has Its Economy Grown and How Big Is It Compared with the USA?" (Paper Presented at the University of Queensland, December 2006): 11-12.

[31] Jefferson, Rawski, and ZHENG, "Chinese Industrial Productivity," 146-180.

[32] XU, "Several Measures Regarding China's Statistics Reform and Infrastructure"; QI et al., "Strengthen Grassroots Statistics Work," 43-44.

[33] Carsten A. Holz, "China's Statistical System in Transition: Challenges, Data Problems, and Institutional Innovations," Review of Income and Wealth 50:3 (September 2004): 404.

[34] XU, "Several Measures Regarding China's Statistics Reform and Infrastructure."

[35] Holz, "China's Statistical System in Transition," 387-91.

[36] Anonymous, "Tongji de Shengming zaiyu Zhenshi [The Lifeblood of Statistics Is in Their Authenticity]," *Tongji Fanglue* (Statistical Policy) 2 (2008): 6-7.

[37] XU, "Several Measures Regarding China's Statistics Reform and Infrastructure"; Jianmei QI et al., "Strengthen Grassroots Statistics Work," 43-44.

[38] XU, "The Establishment, Reform and Development of China's National Economic Accounting System".

[39] Sheng ZHE, "Xiang Xujia Tongji Kaidao (Dealing with False Statistics)," *Zhejiang Renda* (Journal of the Zhejiang Provincial People's Congress) 7 (2009): 31-32.

[40] Gregory C. Chow. "Chinese Statistics," *The American Statistician* 40:3 (August 1986): 191-196.

[41] "An Aberrant Abacus," *The Economist*, May 1, 2008.

[42] The IMF 's report on The Technical Assistance Evaluation Mission to The People's Republic of China is available on http://www.imf.org/external/np/pp/eng/2009/111109.pdf, (last visited on April 7, 2010).

[43] Derek Scissors, *How the Party Says China's Economy is Doing*. Heritage Foundation, July 13, 2012. Retrieved from http://blog.heritage.org/2012/07/13/how-the-party-says-chinas-economy-is-doing/.

[44] Angus Maddison, *China's Economic Performance in the Long Run* (OECD Development Center Studies, 2007): 157, 165.

[45] Xu Xianchun, "Zhongguo Guomin Jingji Hesuan Tixi de Jianli, Gaige he Fazhan [The Establishment, Reform and Development of China's National Economic Accounting System]." Zhongguo Shehui Kexue (China Social Science) 6 (2009): 47-48.

[46] Harry X. Wu, "The Chinese GDP Growth Rate Puzzle: How Fast Has the Chinese Economy Grown," *Asian Economic Papers* 6:1 (2007): 1-4.

[47] Maddison and Wu, "Measuring China's Economic Performance," 15.

[48] Carsten A. Holz, "China's Statistical System in Transition: Challenges, Data Problems, and Institutional Innovations," *Review of Income and Wealth* 50:3 (September 2004): 384-85.

[49] Ibid.

[50] Angus Maddison and Harry X. Wu. "Measuring China's Economic Performance: How Fast Has Its Economy Grown and How Big Is It Compared with the USA?" Paper Presented at the University of Queensland, December 2006.

[51] Yongshun CAI. "Between State and Peasant: Local Cadres and Statistical Reporting in Rural China." *The China Quarterly* 163 (September 2000): 785-786.

[52] Gary H. Jefferson, Thomas G. Rawski and Yuxin ZHENG. "Chinese Industrial Productivity: Trends, Measurement Issues, and Recent Developments?" *Journal of Comparative Economics* 23 (1996): 160.

[53] Rawski. "China by the Numbers," 8.

[54] Holz, "China's Statistical System in Transition," 397.

[55] Orlik, *Understanding China's Economic Indicators*, 24-25.

[56] Holz, "China's Statistical System in Transition: Challenges," 395-99.

[57] Maddison and Wu. "Measuring China's Economic Performance," 14.

[58] Holz, "China's Statistical System in Transition," 384-85.

[59] XU, "The Establishment, Reform and Development of China's National Economic Accounting System," *Zhongguo Shehui Kexue* (China Social Science) 6 (2009): 47-48.

[60] Orlik, *Understanding China's Economic Indicators*, 13-23.

[61] Rawski. "China by the Numbers," 2.

[62] Maddison and Wu. "Measuring China's Economic Performance," 14.

[63] Alwyn Young, "Gold into Base Metals: Productivity Growth in the People's Republic of China During the Reform Period," *Journal of Political Economy* 111 (December 2003): 1220-1261.

[64] Rawski, "What Is Happening to China's GDP Statistics," 347-50.

[65] Wu, "The Chinese GDP Growth Rate Puzzle," 12-15.

[66] Calinoff, "How China Cooks Its Books."

[67] Rabinovitch, "China Figures Prompts Doubts Over Accuracy".

[68] Xia Changyong, "Guan chu shuzi, shuzi chuguan, he shi liao [When does the phenomenon of cooking up economic statistics end?]," August 28, 2005. Retrieved from http://opinion.people.com.cn/GB/ 40604/3648587.html.

[69] Chow. "Chinese Statistics," 196.

[70] Maddison and Wu, "Measuring China's Economic Performance; Holz, "China's Statistical System in Transition," 387-91.

[71] CAI, "Between State and Peasant," 783-784.

[72] Ibid.

[73] National Bureau of Statistics of the People's Republic of China. *Zhonghua Renmin Gongheguo Tongji Fa (2009 Nian Xiuding)* (2009 Revision of the Statistics Law of the People's Republic of China), June 29, 2009.

[74] CAI. "Between State and Peasant," 784.

[75] Xiaolu WANG and Lian MENG, "A Reevaluation of China's Economic Growth." *China Economic Review* 12 (2001): 338-346.

[76] CAI. "Between State and Peasant," 786.

[77] Calinoff, "How China Cooks Its Books."

[78] Rawski. "China by the Numbers," 10.

[79] Rabinovitch, "Chinese Econ Stats: To Doubt Or Not to Doubt?"

[80] Gang Guo, "China's Local Political Budget Cycles," *American Journal of Political Science* (July 2009): 621-632; Victor Shih, Christopher Adolph and Mingxing Liu, "Getting Ahead in the Communist Party: Explaining the Advancement of Central Committee Members in China," *American Political Science Review* 106:1 (February 2012): 166-187.

[81] WANG and MENG. "A Reevaluation of China's Economic Growth," 338-346.

[82] Jefferson, Rawski, and ZHENG, "Chinese Industrial Productivity," 163.

[83] ZHE, "Dealing with False Statistics," 31-32.

[84] Harry Wu, "China's GDP Level and Growth Performance: Alternative Estimates and Implications." *Review of Income and Wealth* 46:4 (December 2000): 476.

[85] National Bureau of Statistics of the People's Republic of China. *Zhonghua Renmin Gongheguo Tongji Fa (2009 Nian Xiuding)* (2009 Revision of the Statistics Law of the People's Republic of China), June 29, 2009.

[86] Deutsche Bank, *China Strategy: Reforms after Leadership Transition* (November 2012): 20.

[87] Holz, "China's Statistical System in Transition," 387-91.

[88] Bradsher, "Chinese Data Mask Depth of Slowdown, Executives Say."

[89] ZHE, "Dealing with False Statistics," 31-32.

[90] Rabinovitch, "China Figures Prompts Doubts Over Accuracy"; Wagstyl, "Measure for Measure: Oil Vs. Electricity as a Alternativefor Chinese Economic Growth."

[91] Calinoff, "How China Cooks Its Books."

[92] Maddison and Wu, "Measuring China's Economic Performance," 19.

[93] Orlik, *Understanding China's Economic Indicators*, 15.

[94] "China to Improve GDP Calculation Methods," *China Daily*, January 30, 2010.

[95] Rawski, "What Is Happening to China's GDP Statistics," 350-51.

[96] Chow, "Are Chinese Official Statistics Reliable?" 397-398.

[97] Peter Ford, "China Reports Solid Economic Growth: Should We Believe It?" *The Christian Science Monitor*, January 18, 2012.

[98] Thomas G. Rawski, "On the Reliability of Chinese Economic Data." *Journal of Development Studies* 12:4 (1976): 438-441.

[99] Bradsher, "Chinese Data Mask Depth of Slowdown, Executives Say."

[100] Roberts, "Foot Massage Doubles."

[101] Keidel. "China's GDP Expenditure Accounts," 364.

[102] Wu, "The Chinese GDP Growth Rate Puzzle," 12-15.

[103] Carsten A. Holz, "China's 2004 Economic Census and 2006 Benchmark Revisions to GDP: More Questions Than Answers," Working Paper (2007).

[104] Bradsher, "Chinese Data Mask Depth of Slowdown"; Simon Rabinovitch, "Chinese Econ Stats".

[105] Thomas G. Rawski, "What Is Happening to China's GDP Statistics," *China Economic Review* 12 (2001): 347- 50.

[106] Simon Rabinovitch, "China Figures Prompts Doubts Over Accuracy," *Financial Times*, July 13, 2012; Stefan Wagstyl, "Measure for Measure: Oil Vs. Electricity as a Alternative for Chinese Economic Growth," *Financial Times*, July 11, 2012.

[107] WANG and MENG, "A Reevaluation of China's Economic Growth," 338-346.

[108] Lawrence R. Klein and Suleyman Ozmucur, "The Estimation of China's Economic Growth Rate." Journal of Economic and Social Measurement 28 (2002/2003): 187-202.

[109] Gregory Chow, "Are Chinese Official Statistics Reliable?" *CESifo Economic Studies* 52:2 (2006): 408.

[110] "Electricity Use Seen Overstating China Economic Slowdown," *Bloomberg News*, August 8, 2012.

[111] Ibid.

[112] Wagstyl, "Measure for Measure".

[113] "Electricity Use Seen Overstating China Economic Slowdown," *Bloomberg News*, August 8, 2012; Calinoff, "How China Cooks Its Books."

[114] "An Aberrant Abacus," *The Economist,* May 1, 2008.

[115] Tom Orlik, *Understanding China's Economic Indicators: Translating the Data into Investment Opportunities*. Upper Saddle River, N.J.: FT Press, c2012.

[116] Peter Ford, "China Reports Solid Economic Growth: Should We Believe It?" *The Christian Science Monitor*, January 18, 2012.

[117] Bradsher, "Chinese Data Mask Depth of Slowdown"; Rabinovitch, "Chinese Econ Stats: To Doubt Or Not to Doubt?" *Financial Times*, June 28, 2012; "An Aberrant Abacus," *The Econoimst,* May 1, 2008; Trefor Moss, "China's Lies, Damn Lies, and Secret Statistics," *Foreign Policy*, June 7, 2012.

[118] International Monetary Fund, *The Technical Assistance Evaluation Mission to the People's Republic of China*. Retrieved from http://www.imf.org/external/np/pp/eng/2009 /111109.pdf; Derek Scissors, *How the Party Says China's Economy is Doing*. Heritage Foundation, July 13, 2012. Retrieved from http://blog.heritage.org/2012/07/13/how-the-party-says-chinas-economy-is-doing/; John H. Makin, *China: Bogus Boom?* American Enterprise Institute, August 2009. Retrieved from http://www.aei.org/files/2009/08/01/08-EO-Aug-2009g.pdf; Roberts, "Foot Massage Doubles."

[119] Tatlow, "The Hiding that Feeds an Income Gap,"; Yiping HUANG, "Huangyan, Zaogao Touding de Huangyan he Tongji Shuju [Lies, Damned Lies and Statistics]," *Caixin Online*, March 2, 2010. Retrieved from http://www.caing.com/2010-03-02/100121819.html; XU, "The Establishment, Reform and Development of China's National Economic Accounting System," 41-42.

[120] For an English-language sample of Xu Xianchun's work, see: Xianchun XU, "Study on Some Problems in Estimating China's Gross Domestic Product." *Review of Income and Wealth* 48:2 (June 2002): 205-215. For Chinese language writing, see: Xianchun XU, "Zhongguo Guomin Jingji Hesuan Tixi de Jianli, Gaige he Fazhan [The Establishment, Reform and Development of China's National Economic Accounting System]" Zhongguo Shehui Kexue (China Social Science) 6 (2009): 41-42; Xianchun XU, "Dangqian Woguo Tongji Gaige yu Jianshe de Ruogan Jucuo (Several Measures Regarding China's Statistics Reform and Infrastructure," *Gaige Jianyan* 10 (2011).

[121] Changyong XIA, "Guan Chu Shu-Zi, Shu-Zi Chu Guan, He Shi Liao [When Does the Phenomenon of Cooking Up Economic Statistics End?" *China Daily*, August 28, 2005. Retrieved from http://opinion.people.com.cn/GB/40604/3648587.html.

[122] Xiaoliang PAN, "Tongjiju Gongbu Quanguo 70 ge Dazhong Chengshi Fang de Chanjiao Ge Tongji Diaocha Fangan [The National Bureau of Statistics Released Housing Price Survey of Seventy Large and Mid-Sized Cities], *Xinhua*, March 1, 2010. Retrieved from http://blog.caijing.com.cn/expert_article-151295-3474.shtml, (last visited on April 8, 2010). The house pricing survey is retrieved from Xinhua News Agency. http://news.xinhuanet.com/fortune/2010-03/01/content_13073997.htm.

[123] Ping LI, "IMF Pengji Zhongguo Tongji Shuju [IMF Criticized China's Statistics with Six Charges]," *Sina Finance*, December 24, 2009. Retrieved from http://finance.sina.com.cn /roll/20091124/21537010433.shtml. The IMF letter is available on http://www.stats.gov.cn /tjdt/zygg/tztg/t20091126_402603677.htm.

[124] Klein and Ozmucur. "The Estimation of China's Economic Growth Rate," 187-202.

[125] International Monetary Fund, *The Technical Assistance Evaluation Mission to the People's Republic of China.*

[126] U.S.-China Joint Commission on Commerce and Trade. *21st U.S.-China Joint Commission on Commerce and Trade: Fact Sheet.* (December 15, 2010). Retrieved from http://www.ustr.gov/about-us/press-office/factsheets/2010/21st-us-china-joint-commission-commerce-and-trade.

[127] "WSJ Blog/China Real Time: Inside China's Gross Domestic Product Data," *Dow Jones International News*, April 17, 2012.

INDEX

D

G

H

I

J

K

L

M

N

S

T

U

V

W